AF705829

TAXING INFORMAL AND HARD-TO-TAX SECTORS

A POLICY GUIDE

JULY 2025

ASIAN DEVELOPMENT BANK

Creative Commons Attribution 3.0 IGO license (CC BY 3.0 IGO)

© 2025 Asian Development Bank
6 ADB Avenue, Mandaluyong City, 1550 Metro Manila, Philippines
Tel +63 2 8632 4444; Fax +63 2 8636 2444
www.adb.org

Some rights reserved. Published in 2025.

ISBN 978-92-9277-355-7 (print); 978-92-9277-356-4 (PDF); 978-92-9277-357-1 (e-book)
Publication Stock No. TCS250268
DOI: http://dx.doi.org/10.22617/TCS250268

The views expressed in this publication are those of the authors and do not necessarily reflect the views and policies of the Asian Development Bank (ADB) or its Board of Governors or the governments they represent.

ADB does not guarantee the accuracy of the data included in this publication and accepts no responsibility for any consequence of their use. The mention of specific companies or products of manufacturers does not imply that they are endorsed or recommended by ADB in preference to others of a similar nature that are not mentioned.

By making any designation of or reference to a particular territory or geographic area in this document, ADB does not intend to make any judgments as to the legal or other status of any territory or area.

This publication is available under the Creative Commons Attribution 3.0 IGO license (CC BY 3.0 IGO) https://creativecommons.org/licenses/by/3.0/igo/. By using the content of this publication, you agree to be bound by the terms of this license. For attribution, translations, adaptations, and permissions, please read the provisions and terms of use at https://www.adb.org/terms-use#openaccess.

This CC license does not apply to non-ADB copyright materials in this publication. If the material is attributed to another source, please contact the copyright owner or publisher of that source for permission to reproduce it. ADB cannot be held liable for any claims that arise as a result of your use of the material.

Please contact pubsmarketing@adb.org if you have questions or comments with respect to content, or if you wish to obtain copyright permission for your intended use that does not fall within these terms, or for permission to use the ADB logo.

Corrigenda to ADB publications may be found at http://www.adb.org/publications/corrigenda.

Notes:
In this publication, "$" refers to United States dollars.
ADB recognizes "Vietnam" as Viet Nam.
Effective 1 February 2021, ADB placed a temporary hold on sovereign project disbursements and new contracts in Myanmar.
ADB placed its regular assistance to Afghanistan on hold effective 15 August 2021.

Cover photo by ADB.

CONTENTS

TABLES AND FIGURES

Tables

Figures

ACKNOWLEDGMENTS

This publication was led by Sandeep Bhattacharya, senior public management specialist (tax), Public Sector Management and Governance Sector Office (SG-PSMG), Asian Development Bank (ADB); and written by Mazhar Waseem, professor of economics at the University of Manchester and consultant for ADB, and Tejaswi Velayudhan, assistant professor at the University of California, Irvine, and consultant for ADB. We would like to thank Agustin Redonda, senior fellow, Council on Economic Policies; Max Gallien, research fellow, Institute of Development Studies and the International Centre for Tax and Development; Donghyun Park, economic advisor (Strategic Knowledge Initiatives), Economic Research and Development Impact Department (ERDI), ADB; John Beirne, principal economist, ERDI, ADB; Luis Almeida, public sector specialist, SG-PSMG, and Hiranya Mukhopadhyay, former director, SG-PSMG, for helpful comments. We also express our appreciation to Tariq Niazi, senior sector director, SG-PSMG, and Navendu Karan, director, SG-PSMG, for their support and strategic direction.

ABBREVIATIONS

ADB	Asian Development Bank
CIT	corporate income tax
DGE	dynamic general equilibrium
DMC	developing member country
GDP	gross domestic product
GST	goods and services tax
HTT	hard-to-tax
ILO	International Labour Organization
MIMIC	multiple indicators and multiple causes
PIT	personal income tax
VAT	value-added tax
UK	United Kingdom
US	United States

EXECUTIVE SUMMARY

- **The aim of this study is to examine the challenges that hinder effective taxation of the informal and hard-to-tax (HTT) sectors in developing economies and to identify practical strategies to overcome them.** It draws on cross-country data, international policy experiences, and in-depth case studies of India, Pakistan, and Viet Nam to assess the effectiveness, costs, and trade-offs of different approaches to expanding the tax base.

- **A binary distinction between formal and informal sectors is unhelpful.** From a tax compliance perspective, an economy's tax base can be divided into (i) registered compliant; (ii) unregistered compliant; (iii) registered noncompliant; and (iv) unregistered noncompliant sectors. A revenue authority's enforcement efforts should be targeted toward the registered noncompliant and unregistered noncompliant sectors.

- **In addition, hard-to-tax sectors, while often registered, also present significant challenges for revenue collection.** These include sectors like agriculture, small-scale retail, and professional services where income is either difficult to track, predominantly cash-based, or subject to high levels of evasion. Taxing these sectors effectively requires targeted strategies, such as presumptive taxation, technology-driven enforcement, and sector-specific compliance measures.

- **Estimates of the size of a country's informal economy do not reveal the revenue potential from expanding formalization.** Revenue authorities should not use estimates of the informal economy as guides to direct tax enforcement efforts toward expanding registration as they are unreliable estimates of what they intend to measure; do not directly measure revenue potential, which is what revenue authorities should target; and do not consider the cost of enforcement.

- **How should a revenue authority allocate its enforcement effort to noncompliant and hard-to-tax sectors?** The answer depends on the net returns from allocating a unit of enforcement toward each of these sectors. Absent any externalities, at the optimum the marginal net return of a unit of enforcement allocated to each sector must be equal. This ensures an efficient and balanced enforcement strategy that maximizes overall compliance and revenue.

- **Net returns of bringing an informal firm into the formal sector depend on four factors.** These are (i) the tax revenue generated by the firm once formalized; (ii) the nontax benefit of formalization, such as enhanced firm growth, improved fairness of the tax system, and positive impacts on tax morale; (iii) the compliance costs incurred by the firm; and (iv) the administrative costs borne by the government. Balancing the social value of these costs and benefits is critical for designing efficient and effective policies to encourage formalization.

- **Existing evidence shows that the tax benefit of formalizing a firm is often insignificant.** One of the case studies presented shows that between 2014 and 2021, Pakistan tripled the size of its formal sector. The expansion of the tax base, however, did not translate into a corresponding increase in revenue: by 2021, the country was collecting nearly the same amount of tax revenue as it had in 2007. Similar patterns have been observed in other countries.

- **Large-scale efforts to formalize the informal sector could still be optimal if nontax benefits of formalization are substantial.** However, the evidence on these nontax benefits is mixed. To date, no study has conclusively demonstrated that formalization leads to significant long-term improvements in either firm growth or tax morale. This uncertainty calls for careful evaluation of formalization policies to ensure that their costs are justified by tangible and measurable benefits.

- **To the extent that the tax and nontax benefits of taxing the informal sector are not substantial, large-scale campaigns to formalize the sector are unlikely to be optimal.** This is because the social value of costs of doing so, i.e., compliance and administrative costs, often outweigh benefits.

- **A firm will voluntarily move from the informal sector to the formal sector if the after-tax profit from operating formally exceeds the profit from operating informally.** While firms in the formal sector are subject to taxes, operating formally also offers many advantages. Formal firms, for instance, can use superior production technology, serve bigger markets, and enjoy better protection under the law. Such organic movement of firms from the informal to formal sector is critical for the development of a country's fiscal capacity. Governments can take many steps to accelerate this transition by reducing barriers to formalization and enhancing its benefits.

- **Smart enforcement can help governments unlock revenue potential from the informal, noncompliant, and hard-to-tax sectors by enabling targeted, data-driven enforcement strategies that maximize returns.** By leveraging big data and advanced analytics, tax authorities can identify high-risk sectors both inside and outside the formal sector. Machine learning algorithms can analyze patterns of noncompliance, prioritize audits, and predict areas where enforcement will yield the highest revenue. This approach allows governments to allocate limited enforcement resources efficiently, focusing on sectors with significant tax gaps or high evasion rates.

- **In addition to smart enforcement, several other strategies can be used to tax the informal, noncompliant, and hard-to-tax sectors.** Simplifying tax registration and compliance processes can lower entry barriers for informal firms, while tailored presumptive tax regimes can provide a practical solution for taxing small businesses with limited capacity for detailed bookkeeping. Leveraging technology, such as digital payment systems and electronic invoicing, can improve transparency and traceability of transactions, making it harder for noncompliance to persist. These strategies, combined with consistent engagement and education campaigns, can build trust and compliance among taxpayers, broadening the tax base sustainably.

CHAPTER 1

Informal and Hard-to-Tax Sectors in Asia and the Pacific

The informal sector has been a focal concern in the efforts to improve taxation in developing countries. One reason the issue remains evergreen is that very little consensus on its definition and therefore its size and importance has been reached. The approach of this publication begins with the principle that the goal of a tax system should be to raise revenue while balancing the objectives of production efficiency and equity. Taking this perspective, this publication will examine what constitutes the informal and hard-to-tax (HTT) sectors, and the gap between beliefs and evidence on their revenue potential.

There is a distinction between the informal and HTT sectors and the underlying amount of their potential tax revenue. HTT does not correspond to groups with the highest prevalence of tax evasion or the largest potential revenue gain from enforcement or base expansion. A broadly agreed-upon definition of the term is activities or groups who can very easily evade taxes or are administratively costly to tax. For example, agricultural income is considered HTT because agricultural landholdings are small. However, Alm et al. (2005) state that, "There appears to be consensus also that the more sophisticated HTT activities, such as electronic commerce or multinational corporations with highly mobile capital and sophisticated transfer pricing activities, should not be considered part of the HTT." If so, it seems that the consensus is that the HTT excludes the hardest to tax and perhaps the group with greatest revenue potential.

Similarly, informal does not always mean noncompliant and formal does not always mean compliant.[1] A broad definition of informal seems to be activities or entities that have market value but are unregistered under any regulatory body, or registered entities that are nevertheless underreporting their activity. Since this publication is concerned with tax revenue rather than the accurate measurement of gross domestic product (GDP), it is limited to the parts of the informal sector that are unregistered with the tax authority (noncompliant) or underreporting their taxable income (compliant). Even so, entities can be legally or illegally unregistered with the tax authority. Table 1 shows the different categorizations and provides examples of their overlap with tax compliance.

[1] It is also worth noting that informal firms may be additionally subject to informal taxes, as demonstrated by Anyidoho et al. (2025).

Table 1: Overlap Between Informality and Tax Compliance

	Formal	Informal	Hard-to-Tax
Compliant	Tax-registered; reports and remits tax liability truthfully	Legally unregistered (outside of tax base), e.g., smaller than mandatory value-added tax exemption threshold	For example, agriculture, microenterprises
Noncompliant	Tax-registered but underreports tax liability or delinquent in payments	Illegally unregistered	Professional services

Source: Asian Development Bank.

Addressing the compliant forms of informality or HTT sectors requires changing the legal requirements for tax registration or changing the tax base, e.g., reducing the value-added tax (VAT) registration threshold or removing an exemption for agriculture. Reducing noncompliant forms requires an increase in enforcement. In both cases, it must be asked whether an increase in enforcement or expansion of the base will increase the revenue sufficiently to offset the increase in administrative and compliance burden (Keen and Slemrod 2017). Our view is that given the diverse sets of activities represented in the HTT and informal sectors, this question should be posed with a specific context in mind (what country, what tax instrument, what activities) rather than asked generally. But first, an often cited reason to consider the informal sector as a whole and separate entity is its purported size and links to other undesirable outcomes such as low use of formal financial services, lack of credit, and low growth. Evidence on the size of the informal sector and some of the nonrevenue reasons to tax the informal sector is examined.

Estimates of Informal Sector Size in Asia and the Pacific

This publication focuses on 17 Asian Development Bank (ADB) members for its empirical analysis.[2] These are countries where the informal and HTT sectors are still a significant concern. Figure 1 shows the size of the informal sector in these countries as estimated using three different methods. The first two are indirect approaches to estimate the amount of economic activity scaled by GDP using dynamic general equilibrium (DGE) and multiple indicators and multiple causes (MIMIC) methods, which have the advantage of broad country and time coverage. However, the drawback of these methods is that they rely on, and are sensitive to, the many assumptions required to estimate the models (Elgin et al. 2021).

An alternative is to implement a survey-based method, e.g., household surveys from the International Labour Organization (ILO), which ask about formal or informal status of employment. The third series in Figure 1 plots the share of employment that is informal in these countries of focus.

[2] These 17 countries are Afghanistan, Bangladesh, Bhutan, Cambodia, the People's Republic of China, India, Indonesia, Malaysia, Maldives, Mongolia, Myanmar, Nepal, Pakistan, the Philippines, Sri Lanka, Thailand, and Viet Nam. These countries are also referred to as "countries of focus" throughout the rest of the publication.

Figure 1: Estimates of the Informal Economy in Countries of Focus

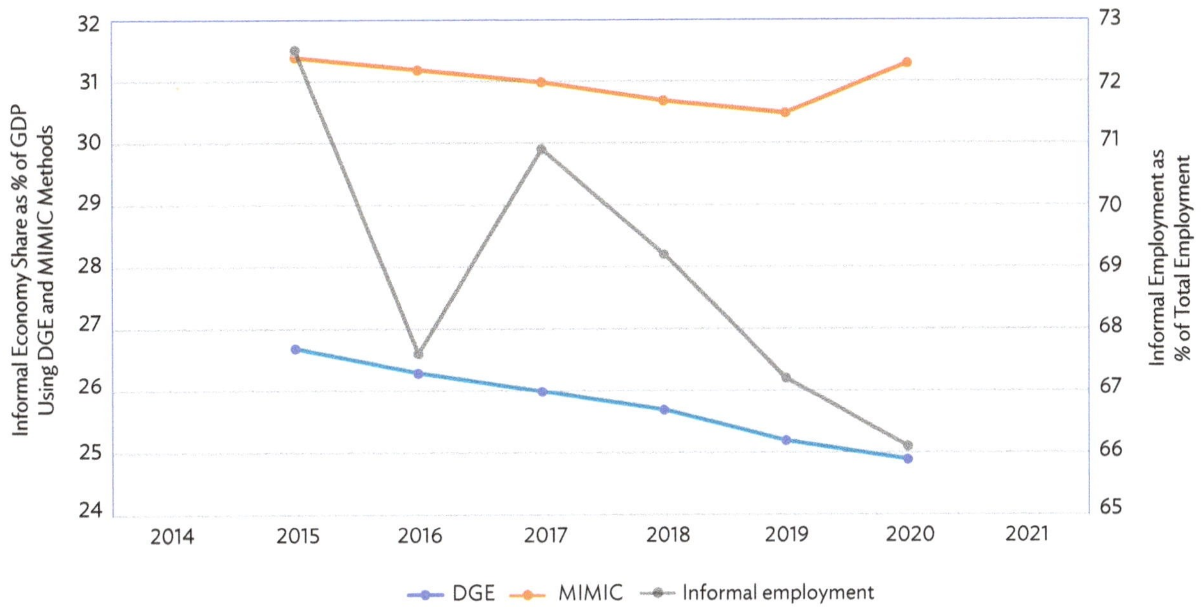

DGE = dynamic general equilibrium, GDP = gross domestic product, MIMIC = multiple indicators and multiple causes.

Note: The selected Asian Development Bank members are Afghanistan, Bangladesh, Bhutan, Cambodia, the People's Republic of China, India, Indonesia, Malaysia, Maldives, Mongolia, Myanmar, Nepal, Pakistan, the Philippines, Sri Lanka, Thailand, and Viet Nam.

Sources: Authors' calculations based on data from Elgin et al. (2021); World Bank. Informal Economy Database. (accessed 13 November 2024).

Both the DGE and MIMIC methods estimate that the informal sector is about one-third of GDP on average in these selected countries. But it constitutes a much larger share of employment—about two-thirds of employment on average is informal. These two figures can be reconciled by the fact that informal employment tends to be much less productive and therefore contributes less to overall economic activity. Encouragingly, all measures show a decline since 2015, although the change is quite small overall. MIMIC estimates have changed only by about 1 percentage point between 2015 and 2020 and seem to have returned to 2015 levels. DGE estimates show a steady decline since 2015 but again have only changed by less than 2 percentage points. The ILO estimates have shown the largest decline from about 70% in 2015 to less than 60% in 2020.

What Is the Revenue Potential of the Informal Sector?

Are these estimates ultimately informative about the revenue potential in the informal sector? Even if all the informal economy became formalized and observable, GDP would not increase by 50%, and neither would tax revenue. This is because, as Zolt and Bird (2005) emphasize, GDP is a value-added measure and so the ratio of gross output in the informal sector to GDP likely overstates its contribution to missing GDP and for the same reason, its contribution to potential tax revenue. Removing double-counting of activities that are not part of GDP (such as illegal activities), the missing amount of GDP is unlikely to average more than 15% at most and varies widely over time and place.

These estimates do not necessarily reveal how much of this activity is untaxed. For example, tax registration and registration with other forms of labor informality are distinct. The ILO estimates capture labor informality. Figure 2 shows the share of the labor force registered for personal income tax (PIT), which is around 40% on average in the economies of focus, indicating that a higher share of the labor force may be tax registered than covered under labor regulations. There is of course considerable variation across economies, as Figure 3 shows. Among the economies with available data, Pakistan has one of the lowest shares of the labor force in the PIT register at 7.6%, while Viet Nam has more registered taxpayers than individuals in the labor force.[3] These differences are likely driven by the requirements for registration and the benefits from doing so. In Viet Nam, even the lowest tax bracket is subject to a 5% income tax, unlike in most other economies that exempt those with income below a threshold.

Figure 2: Active Taxpayers in Personal Income Tax Register as Share of Labor Force

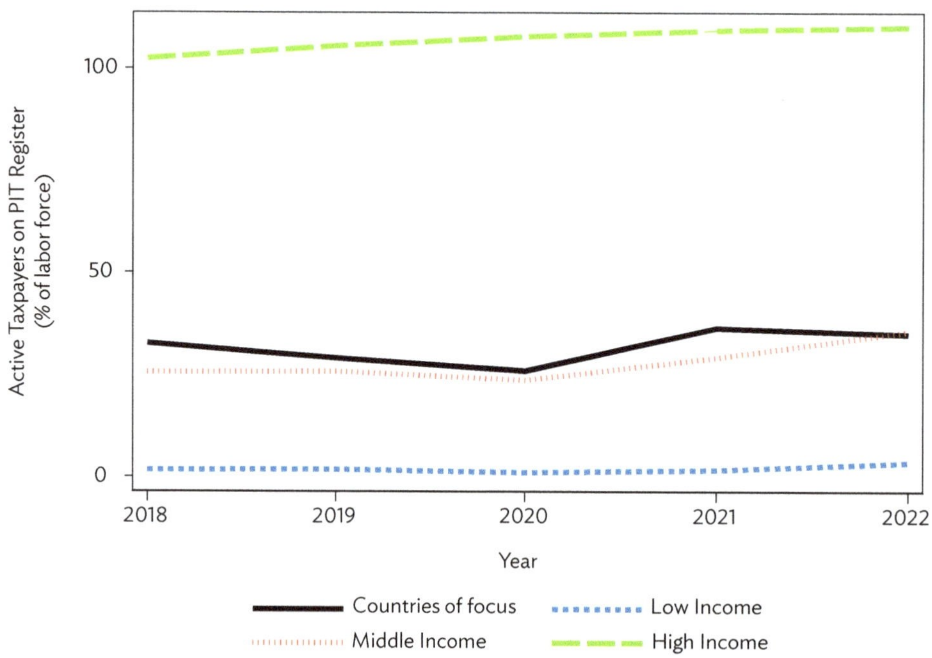

PIT = personal income tax.

Note: The countries of focus are selected Asian Development Bank members where informality and hard-to-tax sectors are a significant concern.

Source: Authors' calculations using data from the Inter-American Center of Tax Administrations, the Fiscal Affairs Department of the International Monetary Fund, the Intra-European Organisation of Tax Administrations, and the Organisation for Economic Co-operation and Development. International Survey on Revenue Administration for 2020, 2021, 2022, and 2024 (accessed 13 November 2024).

[3] Registration for PIT will include many individuals who are not in the labor force but have taxable income from other sources.

Figure 3: Active Taxpayers in Personal Income Tax Register as Share of Labor Force in Selected Economies

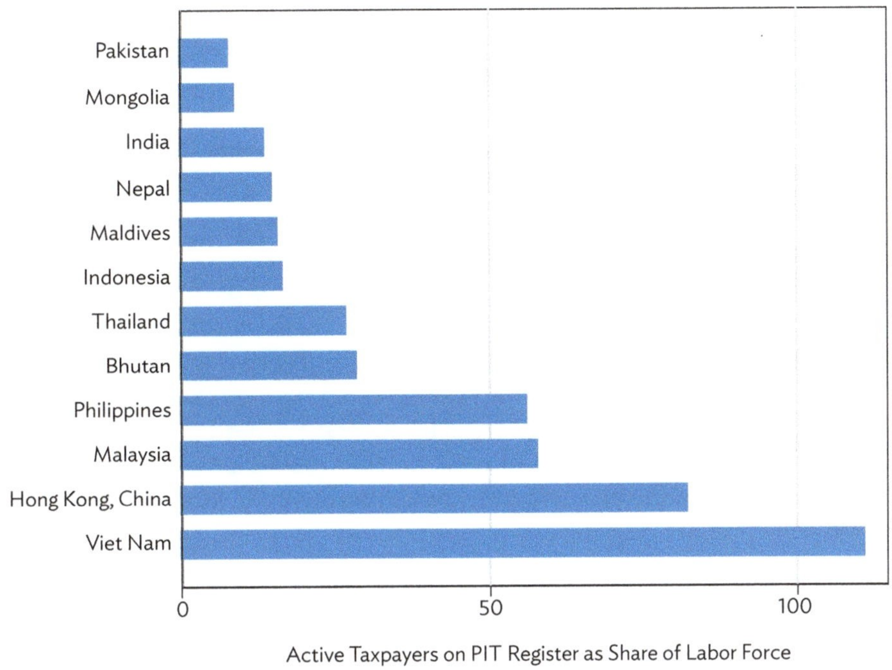

PIT = personal income tax.

Note: The selected economies are Asian Development Bank members where informality and hard-to-tax sectors are a significant concern, and in this figure where data is available on active taxpayers on PIT register.

Source: Authors' calculations using data from the Inter-American Center of Tax Administrations, the Fiscal Affairs Department of the International Monetary Fund, the Intra-European Organisation of Tax Administrations, and the Organisation for Economic Co-operation and Development. International Survey on Revenue Administration for 2020, 2021, 2022, and 2024 (accessed 13 November 2024).

Individuals who are unregistered for PIT nevertheless contribute to tax revenue through other tax instruments. The economic output of individuals is increasingly taxed through their association with firms. In the Organisation for Economic Co-operation and Development and in developing contexts, at least 85% of tax revenue is collected through firms (Slemrod and Velayudhan 2018; Milanez 2017). Firms employing informal labor or individuals who are unregistered for PIT may nevertheless be registered for and remitting a business income tax, corporate income tax (CIT), or VAT. The employees of these firms therefore contribute to tax revenue and bear the economic incidence of the tax through its impact on their employment and wages. Instead of expanding the PIT base by lowering the exemption threshold, countries can raise revenue from the same sources at a lower marginal cost of public funds by raising the rates or improving enforcement of other taxes.

These considerations make estimates of informality in the labor market a poor predictor of missing tax revenue. In the case of VAT, use of informal labor is unlikely to even be correlated with VAT evasion because wage payments do not affect tax liability. In fact, a VAT has several other implications for the link between informality and tax revenue, which is covered in the section "Value-Added Tax and Informality." For example, tax authorities could still be receiving revenue from the activities of VAT-unregistered firms as they cannot claim tax credits for VAT remitted on inputs (Keen 2008; Waseem 2020b).

The evidence on revenue generated through expanding business registration and simplified tax regimes suggests that the revenue potential of the informal sector that is associated with small, nonprofessional firms may be small. As discussed below, the evidence from more direct measures of underreported income suggests that the revenue potential from improving enforcement on registered taxpayers is far larger.

There are alternative ways to measure revenue potential. Taking a tax system as given, tax gap analyses can identify evasion within a given system or instrument. These estimates capture revenue missing through evasion, avoidance, and possibly exemptions. In Pakistan, the income tax gap for 2022 was estimated to be about 30% of total tax collected while the sales tax gap was estimated to be about 24% of tax collected (Government of Pakistan 2022). In Bangladesh, a World Bank report estimated the VAT gap to be about 50%–60% of revenue collected (Rinaudo 2015). These gap estimates include underreporting by existing taxpayers in addition to revenue potential from unregistered taxpayers. Besides these estimates produced by revenue authorities, some academic papers have also estimated the revenue gap using superior estimation methodologies. Waseem (2020a), for example, uses the movement of the income tax exemption cutoff from Pakistan to estimate that low- and middle-income self-employed taxpayers in the country underreport their income by at least 70%. In comparison, low-income employees underreport only around 1% of their income.

Random audits can reveal more nuanced information about where the revenue potential lies. For example, published reports from random audits conducted by the United States (US) reveal the potential revenue coming from evasion by taxpayers of different income levels, suggesting how much revenue can be gained by focusing on smaller versus larger taxpayers. A study of the US Internal Revenue Service operational audits revealed that each $1 spent on auditing individuals above the 90th percentile of the income distribution yielded $12 in additional revenue, while that same dollar expenditure on auditing individuals below median income yielded only $5 (Boning et al. 2025). These findings suggest that not only is pre-audit revenue concentrated among the largest taxpayers, but tax evasion that can be uncovered by audits are also concentrated at the top. Best et al. (2021) exploit a random audit program from Pakistan to provide similar evidence from a developing country. They estimate that around one-third of all VAT-paying firms in the country engage in some tax evasion. Firms that engage in tax evasion on average evade around 40% of their tax liability. In distinction to the US case, however, the tax evasion rate drops with firm size. Consequently, the revenue authority is better off targeting audits toward the middle and upper-middle of the size distribution.

Although these types of analyses and information-gathering exercises may not have immediate impacts on revenue, they are a direct measure of the object of interest to tax authorities, i.e., revenue potential. Not only can they provide estimates of the size of the problem, they can reveal areas of weakness and allow better targeting of resources. Currently, only Indonesia and Viet Nam produce periodic tax gap estimates for either the CIT, PIT, or VAT, although others have produced ad hoc estimates as cited above.[4] In the section "Smart Enforcement: A Data-Driven Approach to Tax Enforcement," it is recommended that revenue authorities introduce "smart enforcement" into their tax systems. Smart enforcement is a combination of cutting-edge machine learning algorithms that harness the potential of "big data" to target audits and enforcement in ways that maximize the revenue authority's returns from these activities. A smart enforcement system can regularly produce tax gap estimates for all major taxes for the revenue authority.

Nontax Benefits of Taxing the Informal Sector

Putting aside revenue gains from formalizing informal agents, are there nontax benefits to doing so? Considerations of taxing the informal sector include that it will (i) improve measurement of economic activity, (ii) improve democratic participation, and (iii) increase fairness in the tax system. Although such nontax benefits are often cited as reasons to engage in costly registration expansion that raise little revenue, there is almost no good evidence to support this. There is no direct, high-quality evidence on how the existence of informal firms affects tax morale and what evidence there is does not find an association between the two (Joshi et al. 2014). The World Bank Enterprise Surveys ask firms about competition with informal firms and find that about 30% of firms in ADB developing member countries (DMCs) report facing competition from informal firms but only 20% report finding the practices of these informal firms an impediment to business. Formalization may not necessarily reduce unpredictability or harassment by tax officials. For example, see the prevalence of firms paying very small amounts of tax to avoid harassment as registered firms (Hoy et al. 2024; Tourek 2022).

Considerations about measurement of economic activity may be justifications for encouraging formalization in cases where the formalization improves the visibility of tax liability even among previously registered firms, e.g., by providing third-party information on transactions. Although a theoretical possibility, the experience of recent formalization efforts as described in the sections "Expanding Business Registration" and "Presumptive Taxation" suggests that it is not realistic. Most tax registers already contain many inactive taxpayers, and new registrants are often too small and have poor recordkeeping.

Finally, it may be considered unfair that some taxpayers follow the law while others (who are informal and noncompliant) do not. It may also seem unfair for smaller firms to be legally exempt since they compete in the same markets as formal firms. These are concerns of horizontal equity, which may sometimes be inherently contradictory to the goal of revenue maximization and vertical equity. From the standpoint of vertical equity, both for consumers and informal firm owners, informality can be equitable (Gadenne et al. 2024). Fixed compliance costs associated with registration

---

4 See Inter-American Center of Tax Administrations, the Fiscal Affairs Department of the International Monetary Fund, the Intra-European Organisation of Tax Administrations, and the Organisation for Economic Co-operation and Development. International Survey on Revenue Administration.

and the reality of who bears the tax burden in practice make presumptive tax schemes and mass registration less equitable as small firms bear a disproportionate burden of taxation (Hoy et al. 2024; Anyidoho et al. 2025; Lediga et al. 2025).

Does formalization help firms grow? To believe that a firm's decision not to register is suboptimal from the firm's own perspective, it must be believed that there is some failure of the firm to optimize or maximize profits. Perhaps firms are not fully aware of the benefits of formalization or have unrealistic expectations of the costs. There is some evidence that the increased credit and market access associated with formalization benefits some firms. McKenzie and Sakho (2010) find that midsized (but not small) firms become more profitable because of formalization. De Mel et al. (2013) in Sri Lanka similarly find benefits accrue to only a handful of firms but not to most. De Andrade et al. (2014) also find no benefits to the formalized firms themselves. Benhassine et al. (2018) conduct the largest evaluation of a formalization program at a high cost and find no benefits to formalization of firms in Benin, not even to firms that have very similar characteristics to already-formal firms. This is despite providing support in tax preparation and bank services to enable firms to access the benefits and lower the cost of formalization. Overall, there is little reason to believe theoretically or empirically that firms who do not formalize have much to gain for themselves by being forced or encouraged to do so.

Value-Added Tax and Informality

VAT has been adopted by nearly every major economy and most DMCs. It has matured over time in many of these contexts, increasing in sophistication of enforcement and compliance (see Brockmeyer et al. [2024] and Slemrod and Velayudhan [2022] on the performance of VAT in developing economies). Today, revenue from VAT has increased rapidly to account for more tax revenue than all direct taxes combined in low- and middle-income countries (Figure 4). VAT has changed the landscape of informality by

(i) raising the costs of remaining informal;

(ii) increasing the importance of scrutinizing existing tax registers, i.e., removing fake firms from the tax register; and

(iii) creating capacity to tax the informal sector indirectly through the channel of input taxation.

VAT has in-built mechanisms that seem to incentivize formalization. The experience of forced formalization has shown that firms will not register unless they perceive the benefits (profits) from doing so to exceed the costs. An unregistered firm purchasing inputs from a VAT-registered firm faces a tax-inclusive price but cannot receive tax credits on that purchase. As a result, the evidence suggests that transacting with formal firms increases the likelihood that a firm will themselves formalize (Gadenne et al. 2024; Almunia et al. 2024; de Paula and Scheinkman 2010). Many firms that are not mandated to register nevertheless do so voluntarily. Gadenne et al. (2024) show that firms that buy from or sell to VAT-registered firms are more likely to register themselves, regardless of whether they are required to. Moreover, Figure 5, from a study of VAT in the Indian state of West Bengal, shows that once a firm registers for a VAT, they are more likely to purchase inputs from other VAT-registered firms, therefore bringing more transactions into the VAT net. These facts suggest that there

Figure 4: Value-Added Tax and Other Revenue in Low- and Middle-Income Countries

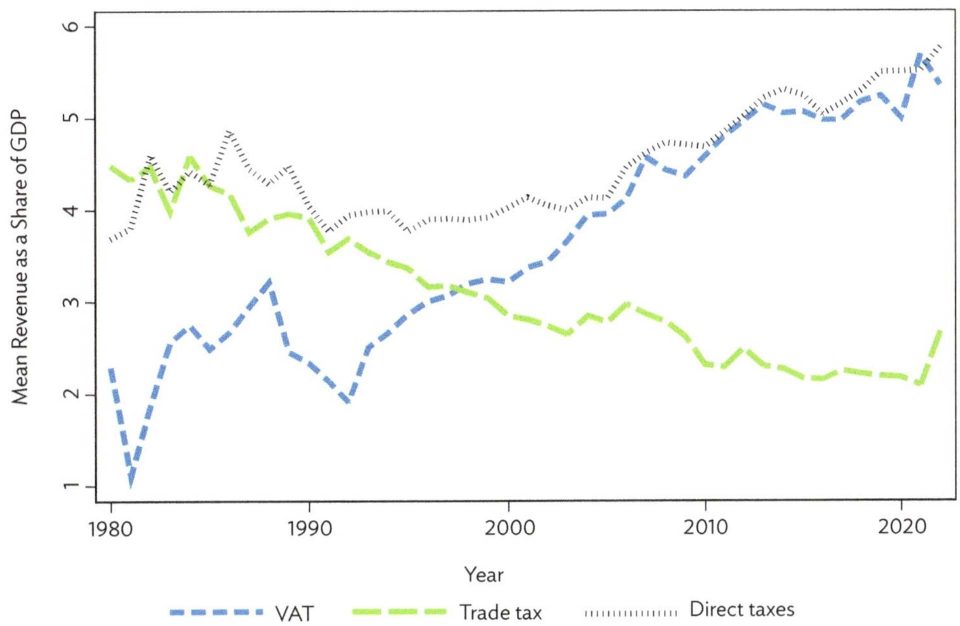

GDP = gross domestic product, VAT = value-added tax.

Source: Authors' calculations using data from UNU WIDER. Government Revenue Dataset 2023 (accessed 13 November 2024).

Figure 5: Supply Chain Dynamics of Formalization in the Value-Added Tax in West Bengal, India

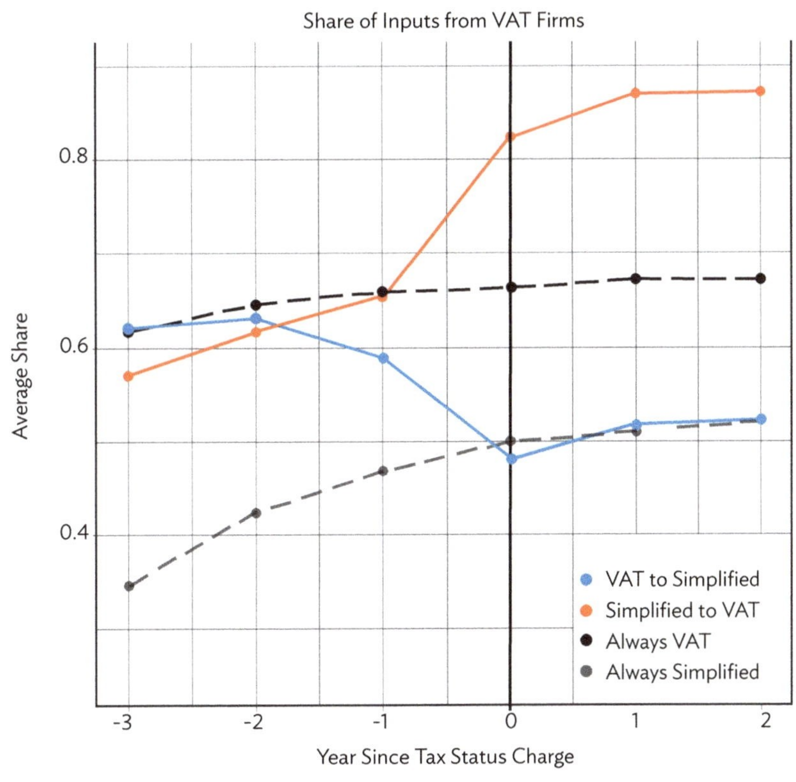

VAT = value-added tax.

Source: L. Gadenne, T. K. Nandi, and R. Rathelot. 2024. Taxation and Supplier Networks: Evidence from India. Institute for Fiscal Studies Working Papers. No. W19/21. Institute for Fiscal Studies.

is unlikely much to be gained in terms of revenue from lowering the VAT exemption threshold. In fact, experience suggests that raising the VAT revenue threshold may be desirable from a revenue efficiency standpoint as described in Keen and Mintz (2004). The revenue gain from lowering the exemption threshold must be traded off with the efficiency loss from incentivizing firms to remain small and the additional compliance and administrative costs incurred. The exemption threshold, like all size-based policies, incentivizes firms to stay small, thereby depressing their growth over time. Bashir et al. (2024b) find that the VAT exemption threshold in Pakistan reduces revenue growth of affected firms by nearly 37%. Qualitatively similar but quantitatively smaller effects are found for India by Choudhary and Gupta (2024).

An important benefit of implementing a VAT is that it can tax the informal sector indirectly. Some of the inputs informal firms use are sourced from formal firms or are imported from abroad. The VAT on these inputs—such as electricity and imported raw materials—is charged and remitted by the informal firm's supplier at the time of supply. The informal firm, however, cannot claim any credit of the VAT paid by its suppliers and thus ends up bearing some of the incidence of the VAT. In this way, the VAT acts as a withholding tax on inputs supplied to the informal sectors, taxing them indirectly (see Waseem 2020b and Keen 2008 for the details of this process). This withholding mechanism had prompted some revenue authorities to use a strategy where imported and domestic input predominantly used by the informal sector are taxed at a higher than standard rate. This strengthens the incentives an informal firm faces to register. Note that a similar impact can be achieved by imposing a withholding income tax on imported inputs and domestic inputs supplied by the formal sector.

Informality interacts with VAT in another important way as well. A VAT contains a built-in mechanism that facilitates tax enforcement, sometimes called the self-enforcing feature of a VAT. Because under a standard VAT the tax paid at one stage is claimed as input tax in the next stage of the supply chain, the buyer has an incentive to ask for the VAT invoice from the seller, reducing the ability of the seller to misreport the transaction. This mechanism, however, breaks down when supplies to informal firms take place. Informal firms have no use for the VAT invoice. In fact, they would prefer their suppliers to not issue any VAT invoice in their name, as it could create a paper trail and may expose them to the revenue authority. On the other hand, a VAT invoice is a check drawn on the government and being so has a market value. This combination of incentives induces some fake firms—called invoice mills—to enter the VAT system. The primary purpose of these firms is to purchase and sell VAT invoices rather than doing any legitimate business. In a recent study, Waseem (2023) finds that invoice mills are a major conduit for VAT evasion in Pakistan. They are predominantly used to claim illegitimate VAT refunds on exports, with roughly 40% of the overclaimed refunds based on spurious invoices issued by invoice mills (see Keen and Smith 2006; Mittal et al. 2018; and Carrillo et al. 2023 for more details on how invoice mills erode VAT revenues in developing countries). Invoice mills are a primary reason revenue authorities must maintain a "clean" tax register, which is covered as part of the discussion of strategies to expand registration.

Tax registers contain a considerable number of inactive firms (Figure 6). The average share of inactive taxpayers on the tax register in the economies of focus is comparable to the share in low- and middle-income economies of about 25% and has remained stable in recent years. In high-income economies, the share is about

15%–16%. These averages mask considerable variation across the economies of focus (Figure 7). The share of inactive taxpayers on the tax register can be lower than 5% in the Republic of Korea or as high as 50% in Bangladesh. The existence of these inactive taxpayers presents a contradiction—why do these taxpayers remain registered while others avoid registration? How can registration drives be rationalized if the tax authority is unable to enforce collection of known liabilities on the tax register or maintain a clean register?

Figure 6: Inactive Taxpayers on Register by Income Group

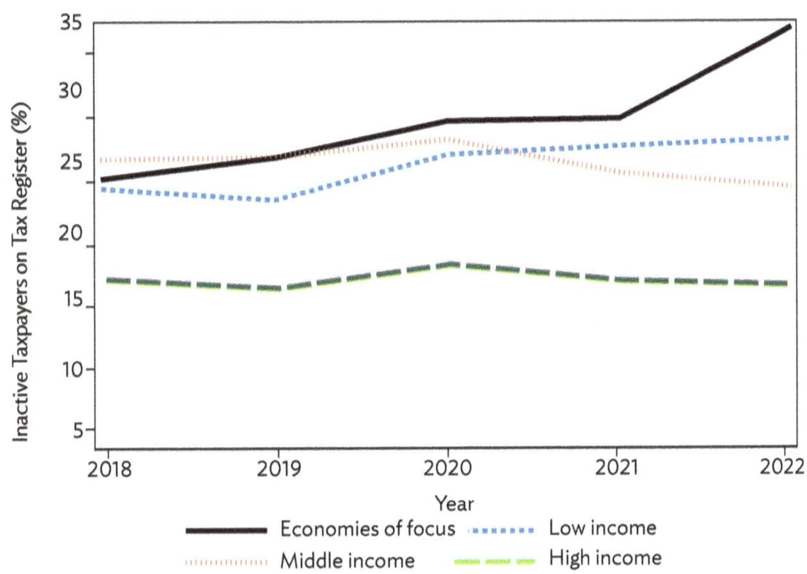

Source: Authors' calculations using data from UNU WIDER. Government Revenue Dataset 2023 (accessed 13 November 2024).

Figure 7: Inactive Taxpayers on Register in Selected ADB Members

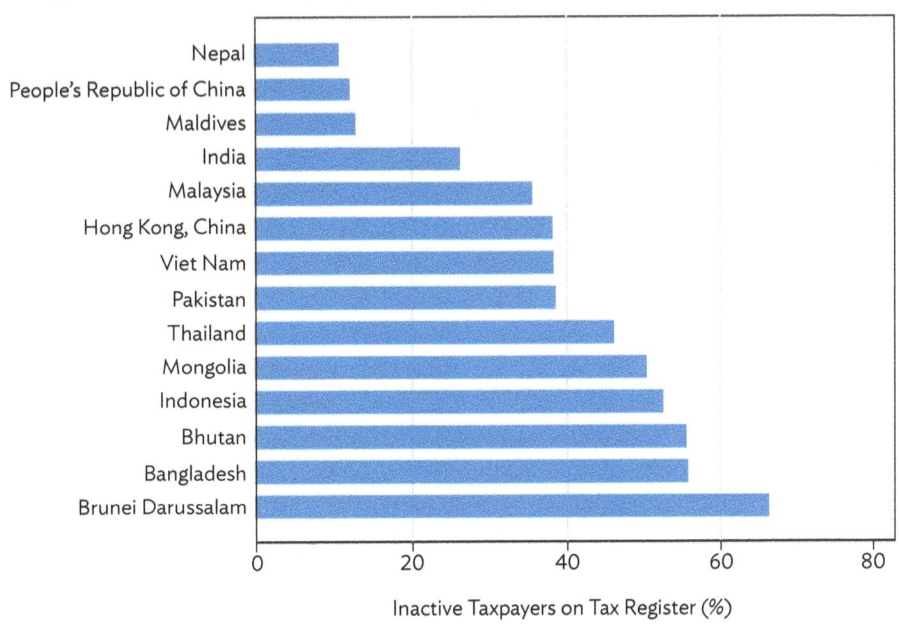

Note: The selected economies are Asian Development Bank members where informality and hard-to-tax sectors are a significant concern.

Source: Authors' calculations using data from UNU WIDER. Government Revenue Dataset 2023 (accessed 13 November 2024).

CHAPTER 2

Challenges in Taxing the Informal and Hard-to-Tax Sectors

Taxing the informal and HTT sectors is important for the development of fiscal capacity in developing economies. These sectors often contribute significantly to employment and economic output but remain largely outside the tax framework, thus not contributing to public revenues. Typical challenges to tax these sectors include issues related to data collection, compliance costs, governance weaknesses, and structural economic characteristics. From agriculture and small businesses to professionals operating outside formal networks, the diversity of these sectors compounds the difficulty of implementing effective taxation policies. Addressing these challenges requires a nuanced understanding of the structural and behavioral factors that drive informality, as well as the systemic constraints that limit enforcement capacity. This section explores the key barriers to taxing these sectors in the countries of focus, using datasets from the ILO, the International Monetary Fund, and the World Bank (Appendix) for its analysis.

First explored is whether the incidence of informality—as measured by the number of people aged 15–64 in informal employment—is higher in the countries of focus than the rest of the world, and whether informality responds to economic development in these selected countries in the same way it does in other contexts (Table 2). Data on informal employment from the ILO and on population and GDP from the World Development Indicators are used. Data are at the level of country by year, 2000–2023. Column 1 shows that on average there are more than three times more people in informal employment in focus countries than in the rest of the world. Qualitatively, this result persists for countries with similar populations (column 2). But the result disappears when the level of development is controlled for (column 3). In fact, when comparing contexts with similar GDP, on average, the selected countries have a significantly lower incidence of informality than the rest of the world. Column 3 also shows that the elasticity of informal employment with respect to GDP is quite large. On average, a 1% increase in GDP leads to a more than 1% reduction in the number of people in informal employment.

A concerning development for the countries of focus is that, in recent years, it is no longer the case that, conditional on population and GDP, the level of informality is lower across these study countries than the rest of the world (compare columns 4 and 5 of Table 2). This suggests that in recent years, other economies have had more success in curtailing informality than the countries of focus. The last two columns of the table include the country and year fixed effects, and the interpretation of coefficients changes accordingly. The coefficient on countries of focus now denotes the average within-country change in informal employment among the region relative to the first year in our sample—the year 2000—compared to the rest of the world. Column 6 indicates that informality across the focus countries has decreased over the sample period. However, the next column shows

Table 2: Informality in Asia and the Pacific

	Outcome: Log of Informal Employment						
	(1)	(2)	(3)	(4)	(5)	(6)	(7)
Countries of focus	2.743*** (0.266)	1.153*** (0.075)	-0.186* (0.104)	-0.653*** (0.224)	-0.098 (0.108)	-0.903*** (0.204)	-2.237 (1.367)
Log population		1.293*** (0.029)	2.258*** (0.032)	2.239*** (0.077)	2.284*** (0.033)	1.304*** (0.212)	1.300*** (0.212)
Log GDP			-1.018*** (0.025)	-0.934*** (0.059)	-1.062*** (0.025)	0.018 (0.051)	0.006 (0.057)
Log GDP × Countries of focus							0.057 (0.057)
Observations	1,188	1,070	1,069	254	815	1,069	1,069
Country fixed effect	–	–	–	–	–	✓	✓
Year fixed effect	–	–	–	–	–	✓	✓
Sample	All	All	All	(2000–2010)	(2011–2023)	All	All

– = data not applicable, GDP = gross domestic product.

Notes:

1. The countries of focus are selected Asian Development Bank members where the informal and hard-to-tax sectors are still a significant concern. These include Afghanistan, Bangladesh, Bhutan, Cambodia, the People's Republic of China, India, Indonesia, Malaysia, Maldives, Mongolia, Myanmar, Nepal, Pakistan, the Philippines, Sri Lanka, Thailand, and Viet Nam.
2. ***, **, and * denote significance at the 1%, 5%, and 10% levels.

Source: Authors' calculations based on data from International Labour Organization and World Bank. World Development Indicators (accessed 11 November 2024).

that this reduction is entirely driven by differential GDP growth in the countries of focus because if one controls for the differential growth, there are no significant changes in informality among the countries of focus since 2000 relative to the rest of the world.

The aim of this section is to identify major challenges in taxing the informal and HTT sectors in the countries of focus. The informal sector is characterized by cash-based transactions and limited financial documentation. In addition, limited enforcement capacity, inadequate data systems, and higher compliance costs complicate efforts to bring these sectors under the tax net. Addressing these challenges requires a nuanced approach that balances enhanced compliance measures with inclusive policies to support formalization, ultimately fostering a more resilient and equitable tax system while maintaining the livelihoods of those reliant on informal work.

Lack of Reliable Data to Identify and Track Informal Firms

A fundamental challenge in taxing the informal sector is a lack of reliable data to track its economic activities. Informal businesses often operate without formal registration or structured financial records, which leaves tax authorities with limited visibility of their scale, revenue streams, and financial health. This absence of data not only complicates efforts to estimate potential tax bases but also hinders an authority's ability to design effective tax policies that are appropriately tailored to informal sector characteristics. Additionally, the mobility and transitory nature of many informal enterprises make systematic tracking nearly impossible. Without robust data and effective identification mechanisms, tax authorities face significant obstacles in assessing, monitoring, and collecting taxes from this sector, resulting in missed revenue opportunities and a tax system that lacks inclusivity.

One of the key reasons that governments of developed economies can tax so efficiently is that most economic transactions there leave information trails. These trails, sometimes also called third-party information, are for example generated when a formal firm pays wages to its employees or two VAT-registered businesses buy or sell to each other. The availability of third-party information on these transactions means that the costs of not reporting these transactions to the government are prohibitively high (Kleven et al. 2011; Pomeranz 2015; Naritomi 2019). Third-party information is usually combined with withholding tax, where firms act as tax collectors, withholding tax payments on economic transactions such as wage payment on behalf of the government (Garriga and Tortarolo 2024). Combining third-party information with withholding is the most important innovation tax collection technology has experienced in the 20th century, and it is the primary reason for the development of the fiscal capacities of developed economies since the 1940s (Besley and Persson 2014). The key challenge in taxing the informal sector is that transactions there do not leave any information trails. In addition, the sector is composed of numerous small firms, which obviates the possibility of using firms as tax collectors. This increases the administrative costs of collecting taxes manifold as the government must collect taxes from many small agents with no verifiable third-party information available on the volume of the tax base involved.

Figure 8 assesses this challenge in the countries of focus. In general, digital transactions—payments through a debit or a credit card—leave information trails, whereas cash transactions do not. Accordingly, information trails in an economy are proxied by the probability that a typical person in the economy owns a debit or a credit card. Figure 8A compares the countries of focus with the rest of the world, dividing them into income groups based on World Bank classification. On average, the countries of focus lie between upper middle- and lower middle-income countries. Less than a quarter of their adults owned a debit or a credit card in 2011, but this proportion nearly doubled over the next 10 years. Notwithstanding this impressive growth, these study countries still lag far behind high-income economies in terms of access to digital payments. Figure 8B looks at the study countries where debit or credit card ownership among adults was lowest in 2011, and shows varying levels of growth in ownership by 2021. Of these, some countries, such as Indonesia, Malaysia, Sri Lanka, and Viet Nam, have made impressive strides in improving access to digital payments, while others, such as Afghanistan, Bangladesh, and Pakistan, still lag behind. Table 3 explores the traceability of transactions in the countries of focus in more detail.

Six different measures for the use of formal banking channels are examined and the countries of focus are compared with the rest of the world. Panel A of the table makes the raw comparison, while panel B makes a more like-to-like comparison by conditioning on the population and level of development. On average, the countries of focus have lower penetration of internet, lower population with a bank or mobile money account, and lower population owning a debit or credit card. These data illustrate a critical constraint on the ability of the government to enforce taxes on the informal sector. The lack of access to formal banking channels means that most

Figure 8: Proportion of Adults Owning a Debit or Credit Card

A: Countries of Focus Versus the Rest of the World

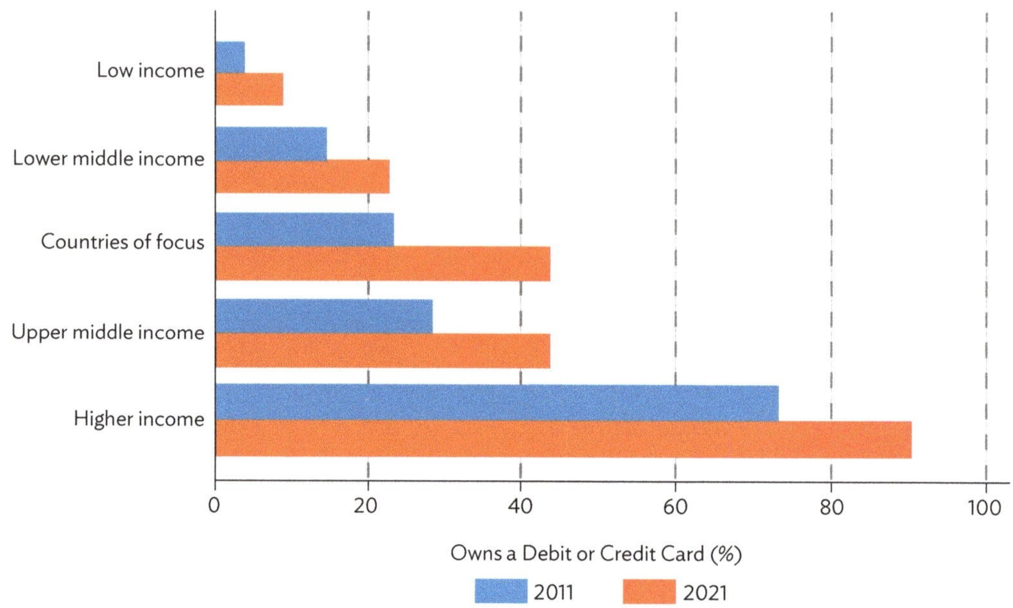

B: Countries of Focus With Lower Card Ownership

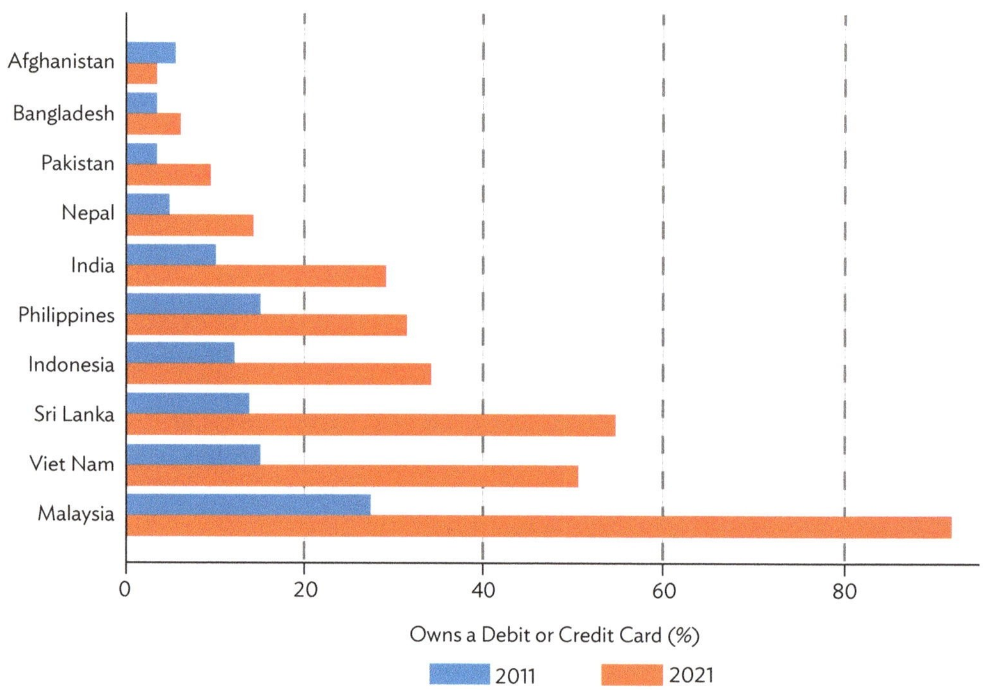

Note: The countries of focus are selected Asian Development Bank members where the informal and hard-to-tax sectors are still a significant concern. These include Afghanistan, Bangladesh, Bhutan, Cambodia, the People's Republic of China, India, Indonesia, Malaysia, Maldives, Mongolia, Myanmar, Nepal, Pakistan, the Philippines, Sri Lanka, Thailand, and Viet Nam.

Source: World Bank. The Global Findex Database 2021: Financial Inclusion, Digital Payments, and Resilience in the Age of COVID-19 (accessed 11 November 2024).

Table 3: Traceability of Transactions

	Individuals Using the Internet (%)	Mobile Cellular Subscription (per 100 people)	Firms Using Banks for Investment (%)	Population With a Bank Account (%)	Population With a Mobile Money Account (%)	Population With a Debit or Credit Card (%)
	(1)	(2)	(3)	(4)	(5)	(6)
A: Without Controls						
Countries of focus	-6.675*** (1.246)	0.581 (2.678)	2.009 (2.840)	-0.025 (0.039)	-0.052** (0.026)	-0.102*** (0.038)
Constant	28.647	57.556	24.446	0.573	0.159	0.439
Observations	6,404	6,470	443	567	232	567
B: With Controls						
Countries of focus	-4.276 (1.489)	9.599*** (3.588)	-0.022 (3.166)	-0.024 (0.045)	-0.045 (0.031)	-0.087** (0.043)
Population	-0.035*** (0.003)	-0.056*** (0.006)	-0.006 (0.015)	-0.000* (0.000)	0.000 (0.000)	-0.000*** (0.000)
GDP	0.006*** (0.000)	0.007*** (0.001)	0.004 (0.002)	0.000*** (0.000)	0.000 (0.000)	0.000*** (0.000)
Constant	27.346	57.453	23.850	0.561	0.163	0.427
Observations	4,353	4,343	381	547	215	547
C: With Separate Post-COVID Years						
Countries of focus	-6.999 (1.401)	5.333 (3.517)	-0.511 (3.663)	-0.051 (0.048)	-0.099*** (0.020)	-0.11099 (0.045)
Countries of focus x1 (year > 2020)	39.558*** (5.291)	37.567*** (11.360)	2.714 (5.925)	0.120 (0.085)	0.173*** (0.058)	0.098 (0.086)
Constant	27.793	57.536	23.855	0.562	0.164	0.427
Observations	4,353	4,343	381	547	215	2222

GDP = gross domestic product.

Notes:

1. The countries of focus are selected Asian Development Bank members where the informal and hard-to-tax sectors are still a significant concern. These include Afghanistan, Bangladesh, Bhutan, Cambodia, the People's Republic of China, India, Indonesia, Malaysia, Maldives, Mongolia, Myanmar, Nepal, Pakistan, the Philippines, Sri Lanka, Thailand, and Viet Nam.
2. ***, **, and * denote significance at the 1%, 5%, and 10% levels.

Source: Data are from the World Bank. World Development Indicators (accessed 11 November 2024).

businesses, especially small ones, must be overly reliant on cash to receive and make payments. Cash transactions are notoriously difficult to track with the consequence that the revenue authority has to spend large resources on the audit of these firms. But even with costly audits, revenue authorities are unlikely to detect the true tax liability of businesses working on cash. But there is some cause for optimism. Panel C of the table separates our analysis by the years preceding and coming after the coronavirus disease pandemic. Encouragingly, across all measures, access to formal banking channels has gone up significantly among the countries of focus since 2020. Over time, a greater availability of information on transactions will have its impact on the informal economy in these countries.

Greater Share of Hard-to-Tax Sectors in Gross Domestic Product

The structure of an economy plays a critical role in determining how difficult it is to tax the formal sector. A greater share of agriculture, wholesale, and retail trade in the economy's GDP presents a major challenge because these sectors are inherently difficult to regulate and monitor. In many developing economies, agriculture and small-scale retail activities often operate in highly decentralized, cash-based environments with minimal formal recordkeeping, making it challenging to assess taxable income accurately. Furthermore, these sectors frequently consist of small, family-run enterprises and self-employed individuals who lack both the capacity and incentive to comply with tax regulations. Wholesale and retail trade often rely on informal networks and are spread across numerous small businesses, adding to the complexity of enforcement. The seasonal and volatile nature of agricultural income also complicates efforts to tax this sector consistently and fairly. As these HTT sectors contribute a significant portion of GDP, the inability to effectively tax them results in significant untapped revenue potential. This structural composition of the economy thus hampers the ability of tax authorities to widen the tax base and integrate the informal sector, limiting resources for development and perpetuating fiscal constraints.

Table 4 compares the share of agriculture in the GDPs of the countries of focus with that of the rest of the world. Although land available for agriculture as a percentage of total land is lower in the countries of focus, agriculture still plays a more dominant role in the GDP of these countries. Column 2 of the table shows that agriculture's share in the GDP of the countries of focus is on average 16.5%, or 4.7 percentage points (40%) higher than the rest of the world's average. This higher share is also reflected in employment, with the countries of focus having nearly 40% more workers in agriculture than the rest of the world. This difference is even more pronounced for male employment in agriculture, which is 60% higher in the countries of focus relative to the female employment in the sector, which is only 37% higher. Unsurprisingly, the employment in industry in the study countries is lower than the rest of the world (last column). Another important feature of these results is that these numbers are quite stable and do not change much if one makes a like-to-like comparison of the study countries and other contexts by controlling for the population and level of development.

Table 4: Share of the Agriculture Sector

	Agricultural Land (% of land)	Agricultural Value-Added (% of GDP)	Employment in Agriculture (% of employment) Total	Employment in Agriculture (% of employment) Male	Employment in Agriculture (% of employment) Female	Employment in Industry (% of employment)
	(1)	(2)	(3)	(4)	(5)	(6)
A: Without Controls						
Countries of focus	-6.675***	0.581	2.009	-0.025	-0.052**	-0.102***
	(1.246)	(2.678)	(2.840)	(0.039)	(0.026)	(0.038)
Constant	28.647	57.556	24.446	0.573	0.159	0.439
Observations	6,404	6,470	443	567	232	567
B: With Controls						
Countries of focus	-4.276	9.599***	-0.022	-0.024	-0.045	-0.087**
	(1.489)	(3.588)	(3.166)	(0.045)	(0.031)	(0.043)
Population	-0.035***	-0.056***	-0.006	-0.000*	0.000	-0.000***
	(0.003)	(0.006)	(0.015)	(0.000)	(0.000)	(0.000)
GDP	0.006***	0.007***	0.004	0.000***	0.000	0.000***
	(0.000)	(0.001)	(0.002)	(0.000)	(0.000)	(0.000)
Constant	27.346	57.453	23.850	0.561	0.163	0.427
Observations	4,353	4,343	381	547	215	547

GDP = gross domestic product.

Notes:
1. The countries of focus are selected Asian Development Bank members where the informal and hard-to-tax sectors are still a significant concern. These include Afghanistan, Bangladesh, Bhutan, Cambodia, the People's Republic of China, India, Indonesia, Malaysia, Maldives, Mongolia, Myanmar, Nepal, Pakistan, the Philippines, Sri Lanka, Thailand, and Viet Nam.
2. ***, **, and * denote significance at the 1%, 5%, and 10% levels.

Source: Data are from the World Bank. World Development Indicators (accessed 11 November 2024).

Figure 9 extends this analysis even further. It shows that agriculture continues to play a significant role in the economies in many of the focus countries compared to the global average, especially within higher-income brackets. While high-income and upper middle-income economies worldwide show minimal contributions from agriculture—typically under 5% of GDP—several countries of focus, such as Afghanistan, Myanmar, Nepal, and Pakistan, have shares exceeding 20%. This reliance on agriculture in the countries of focus is especially pronounced in lower-income countries, where structural shifts toward industry and services remain limited. However, some countries, including Indonesia and Viet Nam, show slight declines in the share of agriculture over time, signaling gradual economic diversification. On the other end of the spectrum, Afghanistan and Bhutan have seen this share rise in the same period. These patterns highlight the varying degrees of dependency on agriculture within the study countries and underscore the challenges in tailoring tax policy advice to each context.

Figure 9: Share of Agriculture in Gross Domestic Product

A: Countries of Focus Versus the Rest of the World

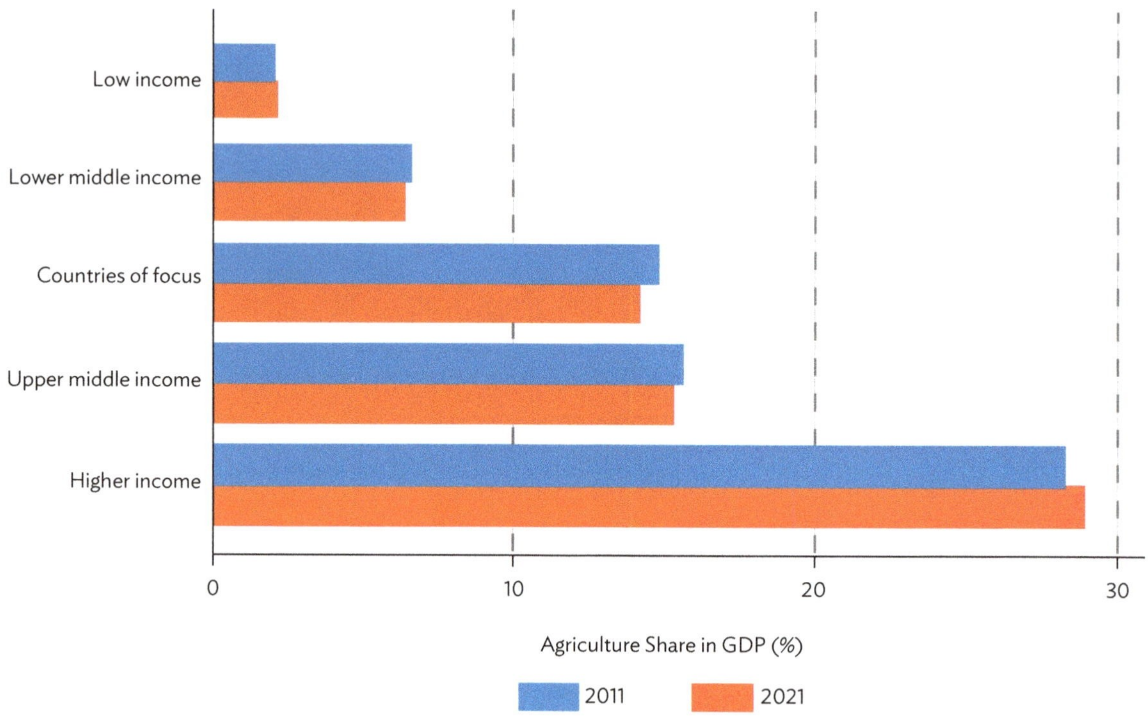

B: Top 10 Countries of Focus With Highest Share of Agriculture in Gross Domestic Product

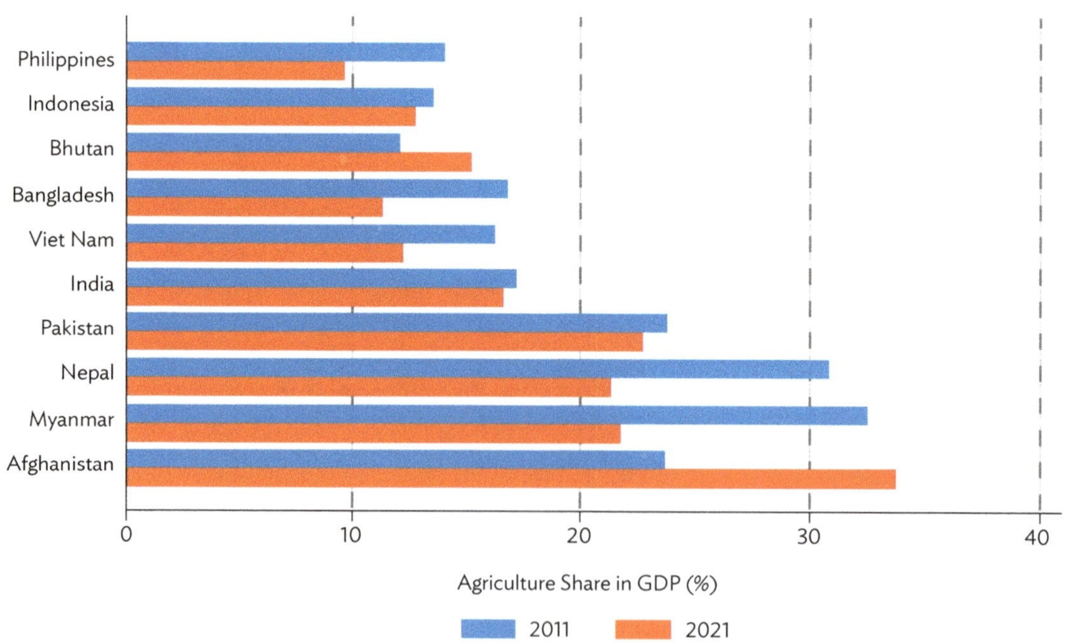

GDP = gross domestic product.

Note: The countries of focus are selected Asian Development Bank members where the informal and hard-to-tax sectors are still a significant concern. These include Afghanistan, Bangladesh, Bhutan, Cambodia, the People's Republic of China, India, Indonesia, Malaysia, Maldives, Mongolia, Myanmar, Nepal, Pakistan, the Philippines, Sri Lanka, Thailand, and Viet Nam.

Source: World Bank. World Development Indicators (accessed 11 November 2024).

High Compliance Costs and Complex Tax Systems

High compliance costs and complex tax systems discourage small and informal businesses from entering the formal economy. Compliance with tax regulations often involves both direct costs, such as registration fees and potential penalties, and indirect costs, such as the time and resources needed to understand and adhere to complex tax rules. For many small enterprises and self-employed individuals in the informal sector, these costs can be prohibitive, especially in developing countries where administrative capacity is limited and tax systems lack transparency. Additionally, small businesses may face pressure to pay bribes to tax inspectors, further increasing the perceived costs and risks of formalization. This resistance perpetuates the informal sector's size, resulting in lost revenue for governments and undermining efforts to broaden the tax base. Simplifying tax procedures and reducing compliance costs could therefore be essential steps toward incentivizing formalization and improving tax compliance. Ulyssea (2010 and 2021), for example, finds that in Brazil reducing entry cost into the formal sector significantly reduces the size of the informal sector and improves overall labor market performance. In contrast, while increasing enforcement reduces informality significantly, it has strong adverse effects on unemployment and welfare.

The countries of focus have a mixed record on compliance costs. This is evident from the results in Table 5, where six measures of compliance costs are compared between the countries of focus and other contexts, with and without controls for population and GDP. Key findings from this analysis are the following:

(i) The countries of focus have significantly lower costs for starting a business. These costs are measured in terms of the percentage of GDP per capita, and the countries of focus on average have 31% lower compliance costs than the rest of the world.

(ii) There are statistically significant differences between the countries of focus and other contexts in terms of the ease of doing business score in both models.

(iii) The percentage of firms visited by or required to meet with tax officials is slightly lower in the countries of focus, but this difference again is not meaningful.

(iv) The countries of focus exhibit significantly higher time requirements for enforcing contracts, with an additional 184.8 days when controls are included. This is a very large difference and is consistent with other measures of rule of law, explored next. Delays in enforcing contracts is a major barrier to long-term investment and may favor connected, unproductive firms at the expense of more efficient ones.

(v) The time needed to start a business is significantly lower in the countries of focus, showing a reduction of about 9.3 days when controls are applied. This highlights relatively efficient processes for business establishment in the countries of focus.

(vi) The countries of focus have a shorter time requirement for tax payment processes, with a reduction of approximately 28.3 hours when controls are included, although this difference is not statistically significant.

Table 5: Compliance Costs

	Cost of Business Start-Up (%)	Ease of Doing Business (score)	Firms Required to Meet Officials (%)	Time Required to Enforce Contracts (days)	Time Required to Start a Business (days)	Time Required to Pay Taxes (hours)
A: Without Controls						
Countries of focus	-30.857***	0.837	-3.405	124.497***	-7.259***	-9.939
	(2.580)	(1.371)	(4.038)	(28.319)	(1.728)	(13.854)
Constant	50.224	61.206	53.262	630.126	33.725	260.357
Observations	2,975	952	358	2,975	2,975	2,692
B: With Controls						
Countries of focus	-31.281***	-2.566	-5.083	182.369***	-9.252***	-29.995
	(3.733)	(1.819)	(4.417)	(34.497)	(1.326)	(18.218)
Population	0.057***	-0.013***	0.049*	0.373***	0.034***	0.308***
	(0.019)	(0.004)	(0.029)	(0.118)	(0.007)	(0.080)
GDP	-0.009***	0.002***	-0.013***	-0.030***	-0.004***	-0.019***
	(0.002)	(0.000)	(0.005)	(0.006)	(0.001)	(0.004)
Constant	52.931	64.374	55.239	608.633	31.136	283.309
Observations	2,205	670	299	2,205	2,205	1,976

GDP = gross domestic product.

Notes:

1. The countries of focus are selected Asian Development Bank members where the informal and hard-to-tax sectors are still a significant concern. These include Afghanistan, Bangladesh, Bhutan, Cambodia, the People's Republic of China, India, Indonesia, Malaysia, Maldives, Mongolia, Myanmar, Nepal, Pakistan, the Philippines, Sri Lanka, Thailand, and Viet Nam.
2. ***, **, and * denote significance at the 1%, 5%, and 10% levels.

Source: Data are from the World Bank. World Development Indicators (accessed 11 November 2024).

Figure 10 provides more context to the compliance cost analysis from the previous table. It highlights that the countries of focus generally have lower business start-up costs compared to low- and lower middle-income countries globally, indicating a relatively favorable environment for formalization. However, significant within-region variation exists, with countries like Afghanistan and Nepal facing disproportionately high start-up costs—over 80% of gross national income per capita in Afghanistan—which poses a major barrier to formalization. In contrast, some countries of focus such as Thailand exhibit notably lower start-up costs, comparable to upper middle-income economies. This comparison underscores the mixed progress within the selected countries, where some countries align more closely with global best practices, while others still struggle with high compliance costs that discourage business formalization.

Figure 10: Compliance Costs

A: Cost of Starting a Business in Countries of Focus Versus the Rest of the World

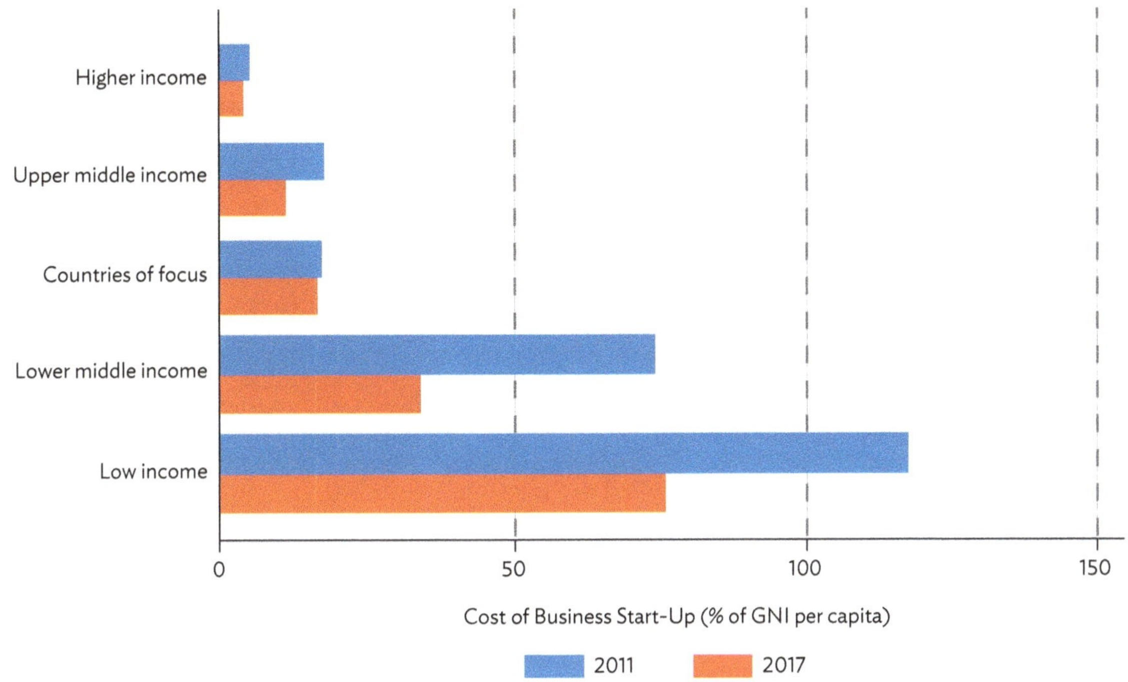

B: Top 10 Most Expensive Countries Among Countries of Focus to Start a Business

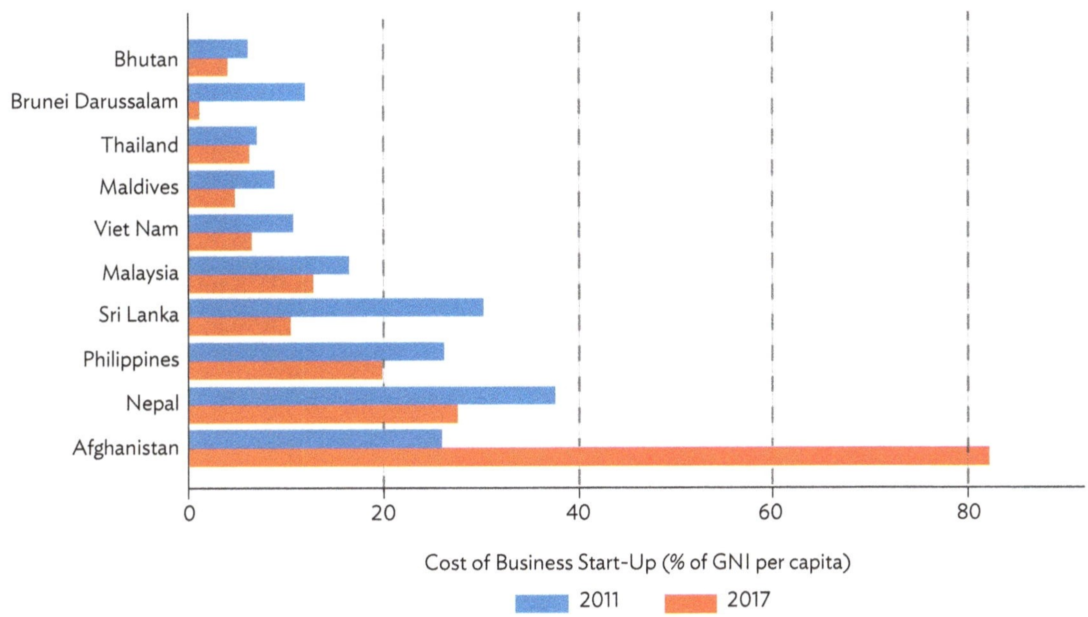

GNI = gross national income.

Note: The countries of focus are selected Asian Development Bank members where the informal and hard-to-tax sectors are still a significant concern. These include Afghanistan, Bangladesh, Bhutan, Cambodia, the People's Republic of China, India, Indonesia, Malaysia, Maldives, Mongolia, Myanmar, Nepal, Pakistan, the Philippines, Sri Lanka, Thailand, and Viet Nam.

Source: World Bank. World Development Indicators (accessed 11 November 2024).

Weak Institutions

Weak institutions create significant obstacles in taxing the informal sector. When tax authorities and regulatory bodies are prone to corruption, businesses in the informal sector may find it easier and more cost-effective to pay bribes than to formalize and comply with tax regulations. This perpetuates informality and erodes trust in government institutions, as businesses perceive the tax system as unfair and untrustworthy. Ineffective governance and poor enforcement of the rule of law also mean that tax regulations are often inconsistently applied, making compliance unpredictable and discouraging formalization. Moreover, without robust institutional frameworks to monitor, assess, and collect taxes, governments lack the necessary tools to broaden the tax base effectively. These issues create a cycle where weak institutions both contribute to and are reinforced by a large informal sector, limiting revenue collection and hindering equitable economic development.

Table 6 surveys the strength of institutions among the countries of focus. It compares six measures of weak institutions in the countries of focus with the rest of the world, highlighting challenges in governance and institutional integrity that affect tax compliance and formalization efforts. On average, the countries of focus show a significantly higher incidence of bribery (about 8 percentage points, which is 54% higher than the average for the rest of the world) and a higher expectation for firms to give gifts, even after controlling for differences in population and GDP. As noted above, the prevalence of corruption and informal payments discourages businesses from formalizing, as paying bribes can be a less costly alternative to official compliance. The countries of focus rank significantly lower in terms of control of corruption and rule of law compared to other contexts, with the coefficient of the focus countries remaining negative and statistically significant in both models (with and without controls). This indicates weaker enforcement mechanisms and higher tolerance for corrupt practices, which reduces the predictability and fairness of the tax system, deterring informal sector businesses from entering the formal tax framework. The countries of focus also rank lower in government effectiveness and political stability, with the the coefficient of the focus countries showing significant negative values. Ineffective governance and political instability contribute to an unpredictable regulatory environment, making it difficult for businesses to navigate tax obligations confidently, further disincentivizing formalization. These findings underscore that weak institutional frameworks in the countries of focus—characterized by high bribery, low government effectiveness, poor rule of law, and political instability—pose significant challenges in taxing the informal sector. Without improvements in governance, efforts to broaden the tax base and enhance compliance will remain limited, as businesses may continue to view informal operations as a more viable and less costly option.

Table 6: Governance and Institutions

	Bribery Incidence (%)	Firms Expected to Give Gifts (%)	Control of Corruption (rank)	Government Effectiveness (rank)	Political Stability (rank)	Rule of Law (rank)
A: Without Controls						
Countries of focus	8.738*** (2.704)	4.662* (2.641)	-8.989*** (1.261)	-0.327 (1.265)	-13.721*** (1.474)	-6.390*** (1.148)
Constant	15.902	16.883	39.915	49.250	50.506	49.860
Observations	372	439	4,783	4,759	4,820	4,873
B: With Controls						
Countries of focus	7.866** (3.066)	0.966 (2.807)	-7.399*** (1.555)	-1.608 (1.598)	-10.173*** (1.686)	-3.151** (1.463)
Population	0.039*** (0.015)	0.046*** (0.012)	-0.034*** (0.005)	-0.019*** (0.004)	-0.038*** (0.004)	-0.029*** (0.005)
GDP	-0.008*** (0.002)	-0.009*** (0.002)	0.005*** (0.001)	0.005*** (0.001)	0.003*** (0.000)	0.005*** (0.001)
Constant	16.955	19.006	37.726	48.079	44.901	46.727
Observations	310	377	3,303	3,298	3,297	3,303

GDP = gross domestic product.

Notes:
1. The countries of focus are selected Asian Development Bank members where informality and hard-to-tax sectors are a significant concern. These include Afghanistan, Bangladesh, Bhutan, Cambodia, the People's Republic of China, India, Indonesia, Malaysia, Maldives, Mongolia, Myanmar, Nepal, Pakistan, the Philippines, Sri Lanka, Thailand, and Viet Nam.
2. ***, **, and * denote significance at the 1%, 5%, and 10% levels.

Source: World Bank. World Governance Indicators (accessed 11 November 2024).

Figure 11 reinforces the discussion on institutional weaknesses. Panel A shows that high-income contexts consistently rank better in terms of the rule of law, with rankings around 80 in both 2011 and 2021. In contrast, the countries of focus and lower middle-income countries exhibit significantly weaker rule of law, with rankings around 40, indicating lower adherence to legal standards and governance frameworks. The rule of law ranking has remained relatively stagnant in the countries of focus over the decade, suggesting limited progress in improving legal institutions compared to high-income economies. Panel B shows that among the countries of focus, there is substantial variation in the rule of law rankings. Countries like the People's Republic of China, Maldives, and Viet Nam show modest improvements, while others, including Afghanistan, Myanmar, and Pakistan, rank poorly, with minimal to no improvement between 2011 and 2021. Afghanistan demonstrates a severely low rule of law ranking, indicative of weak institutional frameworks. These rankings highlight how weak enforcement mechanisms and corruption may discourage businesses from formalizing and adhering to tax obligations.

Figure 11: Governance and Institutions

A: Countries of Focus Versus the Rest of the World

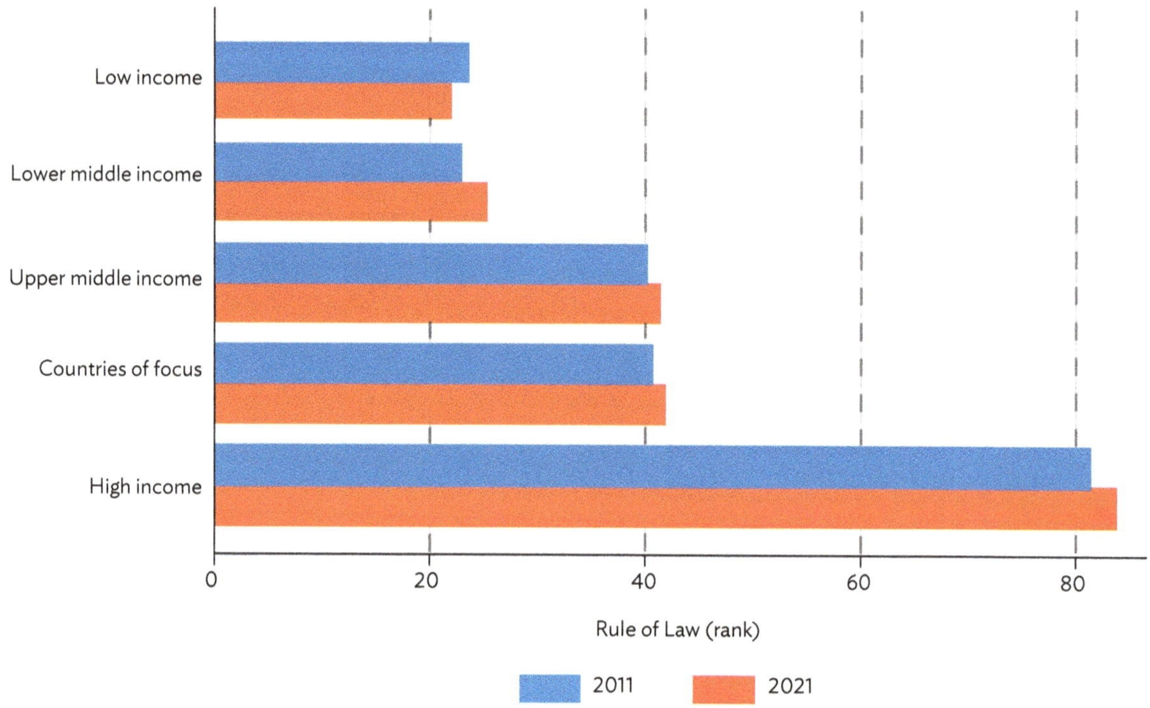

B: Top 10 Countries of Focus

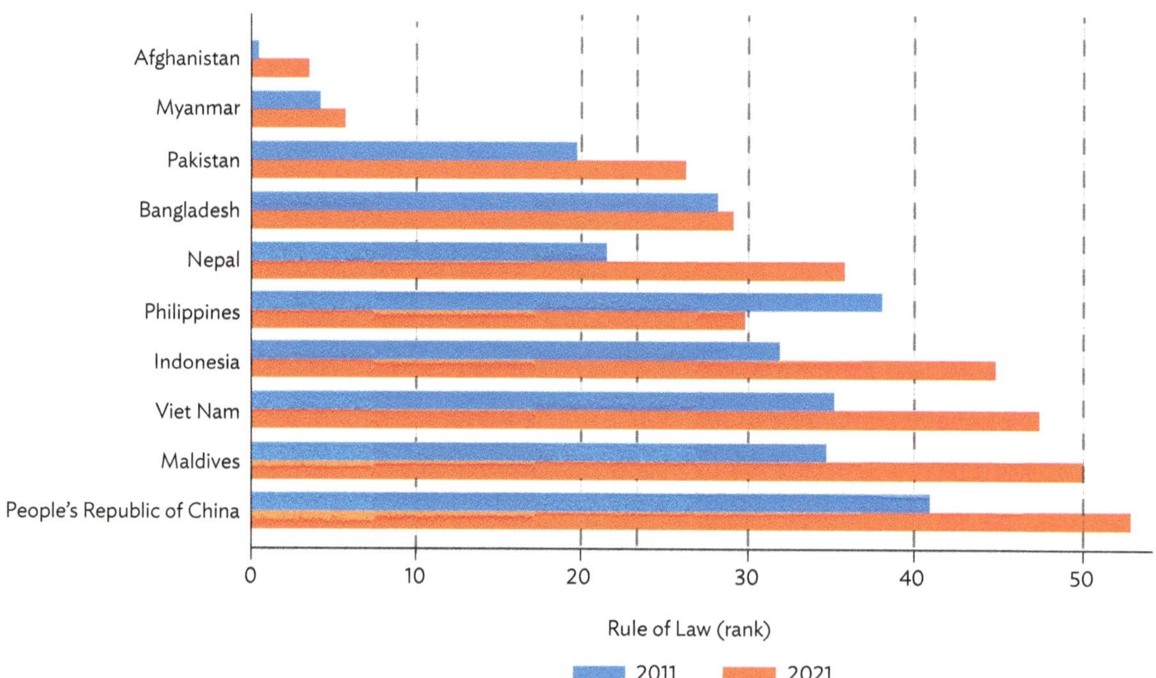

GNI = gross national income.

Note: The countries of focus are selected Asian Development Bank members where informality and hard-to-tax sectors are a significant concern. These include Afghanistan, Bangladesh, Bhutan, Cambodia, the People's Republic of China, India, Indonesia, Malaysia, Maldives, Mongolia, Myanmar, Nepal, Pakistan, the Philippines, Sri Lanka, Thailand, and Viet Nam.

Source: World Bank. World Development Indicators (accessed 11 November 2024).

Barriers to Formalization

Table 7 lists key barriers to formalization, assessing which factors are the most significant drivers of informality globally and among the countries of focus. Our outcome variable is the number of people in informal employment in millions. The outcome is regressed on population, GDP, and measures of the four barriers to formalization discussed above. The table reveals the following:

(i) The share of agriculture in GDP has the strongest positive association with informality. The interaction term for Agriculture Share × Countries of Focus is negative, indicating that in the countries of focus, a higher agricultural share may contribute less to informal employment than in other regions. This may reflect efforts in some countries of focus to formalize agricultural activities or differences in economic structure. Notwithstanding the difference, the result shows that structural features of the economy are an important determinant of informality among both countries of focus and other contexts.

(ii) Weak institutions unsurprisingly contribute to higher informal employment, as poor governance and corruption discourage businesses from formalizing. The significant negative interaction term for Institutions × Countries of Focus suggests that governance challenges are less of a determinant of informality among the focus countries.

(iii) Higher compliance costs are positively associated with informal employment. The positive and significant interaction term for Compliance Costs × Countries of Focus implies that in the countries of focus high compliance costs have an even stronger influence on informality, emphasizing the deterrent effect of regulatory burdens in the region. But we have seen above that while compliance costs in the countries of focus are significant, they are not the worst offenders globally; other regions, particularly low-income countries outside the countries of focus, often face even higher barriers in terms of compliance costs.

(iv) Greater access to formal digital banking channels, proxied here by access to internet, has a negative association with informal employment. However, the positive and highly significant interaction term for Internet Access × Countries of Focus suggests that in the focus countries, internet access is linked with increased informal employment. This counterintuitive result may reflect the unique context of digital economies in the focus countries, where internet access supports informal gig economies or entrepreneurial activities outside formal structures.

In summary, the results underscore that in the countries of focus, informal employment is heavily influenced by structural factors such as a large agriculture sector, weak institutions, and high compliance costs. These challenges make it difficult to integrate the informal sector into the tax base, highlighting the need for targeted reforms to improve governance, streamline compliance, and encourage digitalization within the region.

Table 7: Determinants of Informality

	Outcome: Informal Employment in Millions	
Population	0.344*** (0.001)	0.336*** (0.001)
GDP	-0.007*** (0.000)	-0.007*** (0.000)
Agriculture share	0.198*** (0.003)	0.112*** (0.002)
Institutions	0.027*** (0.001)	0.025*** (0.001)
Compliance costs	0.000*** (0.000)	0.000*** (0.000)
Internet access	0.012*** (0.001)	-0.021*** (0.001)
Agriculture share × Countries of focus		-0.037*** (0.007)
Institutions × Countries of focus		-0.104*** (0.006)
Compliance costs × Countries of focus		0.017*** (0.000)
Internet access × Countries of focus		0.181*** (0.007)
Observations	123,380	123,380

GDP = gross domestic product.

Notes:

1. The countries of focus are selected Asian Development Bank members where informality and hard-to-tax sectors are a significant concern. These include Afghanistan, Bangladesh, Bhutan, Cambodia, the People's Republic of China, India, Indonesia, Malaysia, Maldives, Mongolia, Myanmar, Nepal, Pakistan, the Philippines, Sri Lanka, Thailand, and Viet Nam.

2. ***, **, and * denote significance at the 1%, 5%, and 10% levels.

Source: World Bank. World Governance Indicators; World Bank. World Development Indicators; International Labour Organization (accessed 11 November 2024).

CHAPTER 3

Strategies to Tax the Informal and Hard-to-Tax Sectors

This section focuses on strategies to overcome the major challenges in taxing the informal and HTT sectors. We will explore practical approaches and policy measures that have been successfully implemented in various contexts to enhance tax compliance, broaden the tax base, and integrate informal and HTT sectors into the formal economy. By addressing these challenges strategically, governments can increase revenues while promoting fairness and transparency in their tax systems. Before making recommendations, this publication will address two common strategies that are intuitively appealing and popular but should be approached with caution: expanding registration and presumptive taxation.

Expanding Business Registration

Taking existing tax instruments as fixed, how have different attempts to expand the base fared, particularly in terms of expanding the base to smaller taxpayers? VAT, PIT, and CIT often have size-based exemption thresholds. Noncompliance with mandatory registration requirements tends to be negatively correlated with firm size, i.e., firms that fail to register despite being required to do so tend to be smaller. Both the legal exemptions from registration and the de facto evasion of registration mean that expanding registration necessarily means targeting smaller firms, with lower revenue potential. Several high-quality studies of experiences with expanding registration now show that this strategy is too costly to justify the resulting revenue gains.

The evidence on what works to get firms to register with the tax authority is best viewed through the lens of a tradeoff between the cost of registration and the cost of remaining unregistered. The cost of registration includes a potential increase in tax liability, increase in compliance cost, potential harassment, etc., while the cost to remain unregistered includes a higher risk of enforcement, inability to grow, and even potentially a higher tax liability (e.g., in presumptive tax regimes). The findings suggest that efforts aimed at decreasing the nontax cost of registration are generally unsuccessful while increasing the cost to remain unregistered tends to be more successful.

Interventions in settings across the world, including in DMCs, have shown that the barrier to tax registration is not lack of information or the upfront cost of registration (de Mel et al. 2013; De Andrade et al. 2014; Campos et al. 2015; Gallien et al. 2023a; Gallien et al. 2023). Considerably simplifying business registration procedures in Indonesia did not encourage business registration (Rothenberg et al. 2016).

In Bangladesh, De Giorgi and Rahman (2013) found that providing information about a reform that reduced the time spent on registration from 42 days to 1 day did not increase registration at all. The most successful example of an information provision intervention cost around $1,200 to $2,200 per registered firm, well above any potential tax revenue generated (Benhassine et al. 2018). The consensus is that taxpayers judge the cost of being registered (e.g., tax payments, compliance requirements, possibility of harassment) to outweigh any benefits. Tax authorities therefore will have to resort to enforcement methods to raise registration.

However, although more stringent registration enforcement is more successful, it does not generate much additional revenue. In Sierra Leone, Gallien et al. (2023) studied a mass registration exercise motivated by estimates that around 45% of businesses were unregistered with the tax authority. The registration exercise was performed through physical verification by enumerators at physical locations of establishments. The drive successfully identified many unregistered businesses that would have doubled the tax register. However, it mainly captured smaller, retail establishments, about a third of whom had annual turnover lower than the income tax registration threshold. The drive failed to capture high-income professionals, which were of particular interest. Moreover, most of these newly identified businesses were not eventually registered and did not start contributing to tax revenue.

One might argue that the issue in Sierra Leone was the reliance on costly use of enumerators and physical verification as opposed to identification through existing records such as electricity use. The evidence suggests otherwise. Even increasing registration by cross-checking across tax instruments within the tax register in South Africa resulted in new registrants that did not file or remit taxes. Only 14% of new registrants submitted a tax return after registration and those who did so were unlikely to report a positive tax liability or remit the tax due. This is especially concerning given that this registration method targeted semiformal firms that were larger and more profitable firms than the typical informal firm. Nevertheless, owing to the scale and low-cost nature of such interventions, they can be cost-effective as they do raise some revenue and generate spillovers to compliance among already-registered firms (Lediga et al. 2025).

Uganda's 2021 registration campaign resulted in registering taxpayers who were much less likely to pay any tax than those who voluntarily registered, partly because of the poor quality of data collected. Rwanda's registration drive found that those who are recruited through mass campaigns are more likely to file nil-returns. While "ghosts" exist among business taxation, it seems as though existing strategies have either revealed that they are of low-revenue potential or seem ill-equipped at identifying those with high-revenue potential.

Implementing a VAT has created a problem of fake registrations where firms—sometimes referred to as invoice mills—register in order to provide fake VAT credits without making associated payments (Waseem 2023). This phenomenon raises the desirability of a "clean" VAT register where all registered firms are ensured to be active and making tax payments, and on ensuring compliance among registered firms.

The cost of ensuring a clean register is not trivial. Almunia et al. (2024) show that tax authorities are unable to perform basic cross-checks that ensure firms are not providing excess credits.

A large number of inactive entities on the tax register are likely to exacerbate this problem. Waseem (2023) finds that entities who register mainly for buying and selling VAT invoices are a major conduit for tax evasion in Pakistan. Their primary use is to facilitate over-claim of VAT refunds on exports, with roughly 40% of the overclaimed refund arising because of invoices issued by these fake entities. Barwahwala et al. (2024) implemented a machine learning algorithm to identify fraudulent nonexistent firms that are used for tax evasion in India. Physical verifications of selected taxpayers revealed that 53% of firms identified by the algorithm were bogus, a much higher hit rate than the 4% revealed by random verifications and 38% revealed by the rule-of-thumb used by tax officers. Carrillo et al. (2017) find that tax authority-led crackdowns on ghost firms result in an increase in tax payments by increasing enforcement on those who had purchased from these ghost firms in the past. These examples show how crucial a clean register is to the VAT.

Presumptive Taxation

Taxpayers are also discouraged from registering by burdensome compliance requirements. For example, registered taxpayers are usually required to file returns with detailed information, maintain accurate records, and submit to verifications. Some firms may not be sufficiently attached to the finance sector or generate information in other ways that enable the revenue authority to verify and enforce their liabilities. Presumptive taxation, i.e., taxing based on easily observable characteristics, taxing on turnover, or setting a minimum tax, is a way to generate revenue from the lower end of the taxpayer distribution while lowering the administrative and compliance burden. Registered taxpayers smaller than a size threshold (usually stated in terms of turnover or profit) are eligible for a simplified tax regime with minimal filing and recordkeeping requirements. Such instruments have small efficiency costs and do not raise much revenue, but may bring nonrevenue benefits of formalization and provide a path to voluntary formalization and growth.

There are three margins of response to consider when designing and implementing a presumptive tax regime: (i) registration decisions of firms that would have been unregistered in the absence of the presumptive regime; (ii) firms that are registered in the absence of the presumptive regime but would qualify for the presumptive tax; and (iii) firms that are registered but would not qualify for the presumptive tax based on their pre-reform characteristics, e.g., firms that are above the turnover threshold for the presumptive regime. A presumptive tax that maintains the same registration threshold but simplifies an existing VAT, PIT, or CIT could induce firms to register but could also reduce revenue from the already-formal firms who qualify for the presumptive regime or who are induced to appear or remain small to qualify. A tax reform that introduces or modifies a presumptive tax should consider the tradeoff between these three margins of response.

A few rigorous evaluations of experiences with presumptive tax regimes suggest that they can encourage registration. A simplified regime in Georgia for firms below a given turnover threshold resulted in a one-time increase in firm registration just below that threshold (Bruhn and Loeprick 2016). The increase in registration came from an existing stock of informal firms registering rather than newly created firms or existing registered firms reporting lower turnover. However, how much these newly registered firms contribute to tax revenue was unable to be measured. Brazil's SIMPLES program reduced tax for some taxpayers on top of simplifying registration procedures, which encouraged formalization but resulted in a net revenue decrease (Rocha et al. 2018). The increased revenue from newly formal firms did not offset the decrease in revenue for already-formal firms.

Presumptive regimes do induce firms to remain small to take advantage of the simplified regime. However, this margin of distortion is generally small. Much of this evidence comes from VAT exemption thresholds, such as in Ethiopia (Gebresilasse and Sow 2020), Finland (Harju et al. 2019), Pakistan (Bashir et al. 2024b), the United Kingdom (UK) (Liu et al. 2022). Most VAT regimes have a simplified regime for small firms, and these studies show that firms limit their size by around 10%–20% near the exemption threshold to take advantage of the simplified regime. It is important to keep in mind that only firms that are close enough to the exemption threshold, i.e., relatively small, will adjust their size in this way, limiting the efficiency loss. Still, revenue gains in terms of taxpayer registration are likely to come from even smaller firms making the net benefit unclear. For CIT and PIT, presumptive regimes may be more distortionary since there is no incentive to voluntarily register for the full regime, unlike in a VAT.

Minimum taxes face similar tradeoffs, albeit along a different margin than revenue. Best et al. (2015) show that a minimum tax scheme in Pakistan was effective at raising revenue from small corporations that would otherwise have yielded little revenue from a tax on profits. This result is predicated on the fact that overreporting costs (and thereby underreporting profits) is much easier than underreporting revenue. They find little distortion of real production at this margin, suggesting that the efficiency cost of such a presumptive scheme is small.

While presumptive regimes can have low costs for the revenue authority and taxpayers, care must be taken to ensure that they do not simply act as a nuisance tax that raises little revenue but presents a hassle to the taxpayer. In a recent study, Hoy et al. (2024) find that presumptive regimes do seem to add more burden on taxpayers than previously known, even though they bring in very little revenue. In Kenya, many taxpayers in the presumptive regime did not know their actual tax liability even though it was theoretically simple to calculate if they knew their monthly sales. These taxpayers tended to pay the same fixed amount regardless of the actual liability even if the liability may have been lower. This new evidence suggests that even very simple regimes may be more burdensome to taxpayers than previously understood.

Presumptive and simplified tax regimes are widely prevalent and likely to remain so. They are beneficial in the sense that they provide a path to formalization for growing firms without an immediate, large burden in terms of compliance costs. They are preferable to mass registration expansion since they are less costly for the tax authority to administer and for the taxpayer to participate in. Nevertheless, expanding presumptive regimes by requiring even smaller taxpayers or by raising the exemption threshold come with revenue tradeoffs that should be measured and considered.

Smart Enforcement: A Data-Driven Approach to Tax Enforcement

Advances in technology are revolutionizing the task of revenue authorities in the developed world. These authorities are increasingly using the predictive power of big data to identify unregistered businesses, detect tax evasion, target enforcement, and recover the evaded amounts. In some respects, more data are available to revenue authorities of developing economies than their counterparts in the developed world. For example, transaction-level details of all sales and purchases are now collected in many developing contexts, such as Pakistan. In contrast, no such information is obtained in developed contexts, such as the UK. Data is the most important resource for tax enforcement; developing economies collect vast amounts of data from taxpayers, but they are either not utilized or utilized very inefficiently (Okunogbe and Tourek 2024). One strategy to tax the informal sector and expand the tax base is to harness the potential of big data to identify unregistered taxpayers. An added benefit of the data-driven approach—which we call smart enforcement—is that once it is developed it can also be used to target audits toward the most risky taxpayers, where risky taxpayers include both registered and unregistered taxpayers. The approach thus can be used to combat tax evasion within the registered sector and to fight informality in the unregistered sector.

What Is Smart Enforcement?

Smart enforcement combines tax and nontax data usually available from the revenue authorities of developing economies with cutting-edge machine learning algorithms to address two critical gaps in enforcement capacity in these contexts.

Risk-based targeting. Revenue authorities can usually audit only around 5% of tax returns each year. It is therefore critical that these audits are targeted toward the most egregious tax evaders so that their impact can be maximized. But existing evidence shows that the targeting mechanisms used in developing economies are extremely inefficient. Using data from Pakistan, Best et al. (2021), for example, find that risk-based mechanisms used by the country do not do better than random audits in discriminating the risk of tax evasion. There are many technological and institutional reasons for developing economies' lack of efficient targeting mechanisms. Importantly, they do not have the capacity to evaluate the objective revenue risk of each taxpayer, something which requires comparing the revenue remitted by a taxpayer to the potential revenue remitted by the taxpayer in a world with no tax evasion. As a result, most still use archaic discretion-based rules to allocate audits, and where data-driven risk mechanisms are used, they do not even attempt to estimate the objective risk of each taxpayer. The key innovation of smart enforcement consists of allocating around 10% of audits each year randomly. By combining this experimental variation with data and using cutting-edge machine learning algorithms a revenue authority can estimate the tax gap for all major taxes as well as implement the most efficient targeting mechanism for audit.

Detection technology and recovery capacity. In developing contexts, the detection technology of the revenue authority is seriously underdeveloped. Detection technology refers to the probability that a typical tax audit conducted by the revenue authority would be able to detect tax evasion committed by a taxpayer. If the detection technology of a revenue authority is weak, it cannot for example determine the true income of an informal taxpayer and thus cannot ask it to register. Besides detection, the revenue authorities also lack recovery capacity. Recovery capacity refers to the probability that an amount detected by audit would be ultimately recovered by the revenue authority. With weak recovery capacity, audit detections often remain stuck in prolonged litigation, resulting in delayed recovery of detected amounts and failing to create deterrence against noncompliance. Recent research has found that more than the detection technology weak recovery capacity is the key constraint in curtailing tax evasion in developing economies (Best et al. 2021; Okunogbe 2021). The primary reason detection technology and recovery capacity are weak in developing economies is that governments lose track of recoverable amounts found by audits as they enter the litigation stages. This creates a principal-agent problem whereby tax inspectors are not incentivized to provide high effort as the government does not observe the outcome of their efforts and hence the quality of their detection. Smart enforcement also helps eliminate this problem. It creates end-to-end linkage of the audit-detection-recovery process. As a result, the government can track the outcomes of audits to their logical end, determine the quality of audit, and compensate the auditors accordingly. This in turn weakens the principal-agent problem at the heart of the low detection and recovery capacities.

How Can a Country Implement Smart Enforcement?

Smart enforcement has two principal modules. Figure 12 shows the first of these—the targeting module. It requires making three innovations to the status quo observed in most developing economies. First, it introduces random variation into audit assignment, requiring around 10% of audits to be allocated randomly rather than through the risk-based mechanism revenue authorities commonly use for this purpose. Random audits need to be intensive in scope and their purpose is to estimate cleanly the tax gap for major groups of taxpayers. The next component of the module is the compliance model. It takes as input data from (i) random audits, (ii) risk-based audits, (iii) tax returns, and (iv) a compliance survey, described below. It then uses cutting-edge machine learning tools to predict noncompliance across various groups of taxpayers. The final component of the module—the risk engine—uses the compliance model to identify taxpayers that are most likely to benefit from enforcement. Targeting audit and enforcement toward these taxpayers would maximize returns to the revenue authority's enforcement efforts. The purpose of the compliance survey is to generate data that are not available with the revenue authority from tax returns or other sources but are essential for running the compliance model. Even comprehensive audits cannot estimate the true extent of tax evasion, and one aim of the survey is to find the factor by which random audit results must be multiplied to arrive at the true tax gap estimates. This factor must be estimated at reasonably narrow industry, sector, and firm-size levels. The survey can also generate data on informal firms that could be targeted for enforcement.

Figure 12: Smart Enforcement

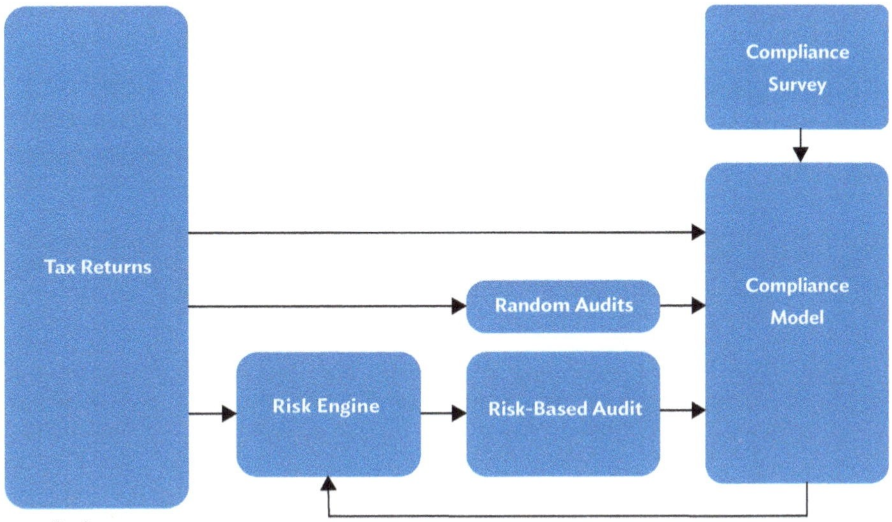

Source: Asian Development Bank.

The second module of smart enforcement focuses on improving the detection technology and recovery capacity of the revenue authority. The key innovation in this module is linking the long-run outcomes of audit with initial assignment. This end-to-end automation of the process chain creates information on the quality of detection. High-quality detections would withstand scrutiny at the litigation stages, leading ultimately to the recovery of the detected amount. Low-quality detections, on the other hand, would be set aside, producing no recovery. This would fix the principal-agent problem at the heart of the existing enforcement regimes of most developing economies, inducing tax inspectors to produce higher effort.

What Can a Revenue Authority Achieve by Implementing Smart Enforcement?

Smart enforcement can enhance capacity of the revenue authority to detect, recover, and punish tax evasion, thereby reducing the tax gap and creating an abiding deterrence against tax evasion and informality. Specifically, the revenue authority can reap the following benefits:

(i) **Tax gap estimates.** Smart enforcement can regularly produce the tax gap estimates of the country. This is a built-in feature of the model and does not require any additional investment or effort by the revenue authority. Once the results of the random audits are fed into the system, it can automatically produce the tax gap estimates for all major taxes in the country.

(ii) **Identification of informal firms.** Smart enforcement can identify informal firms that need to be registered. The machine learning algorithms built into smart enforcement can use transaction-level data filed by buyers and sellers of the informal sector, combining it with the information from the compliance survey and nontax sources, to create potential income of informal sector firms, and identify those that are operating above the exemption threshold level. These firms then can be asked by the revenue authority to register.

(iii) **Targeted risk-based audits.** Because smart enforcement can estimate a firm's potential tax revenue—the tax a firm would have paid if there were no tax evasion—it can identify firms whose audit would result in most tax and nontax benefits, where tax benefit is in terms of additional revenue realized and nontax benefit is in terms of creating an abiding deterrence against tax evasion and informality. By targeting the enforcement effort toward these firms, the revenue authority can maximize the return on its effort.

Smart enforcement represents a transformative approach to tax administration, leveraging the power of big data and modern machine learning algorithms to detect, recover, and deter tax evasion. For developing economies, where informal and HTT sectors dominate, this approach offers a promising solution. By analyzing vast datasets—such as tax records, banking transactions, utility payments, property ownership, and social media activity—tax authorities can identify discrepancies between reported incomes and actual economic activity. Machine learning models can detect patterns of evasion, prioritize high-risk cases for audits, and even predict future noncompliance. This targeted approach minimizes reliance on blanket enforcement measures and large-scale registration drives, reducing administrative burdens and compliance costs while maximizing revenue recovery.

Developed economies are already leading the way in utilizing such modules. For example, the US Internal Revenue Service employs machine learning algorithms to analyze vast datasets to flag suspicious filings and prioritize audits. Similarly, the UK's HM Revenue and Customs uses its "Connect" system to cross-reference data from over 30 sources, including bank accounts; savings, pensions, and investment records; credit and debit card payments; activity on online platforms; motor-registration records; earnings and benefits; social media; real estate transactions; and all tax documents, to detect tax evasion and informality. By enhancing efficiency and reducing reliance on manual inspections, smart enforcement can not only improve revenue collection but can also foster trust and fairness, signaling that all economic actors, including those in informal sectors, are held accountable under the tax system. For developing economies, adopting such technologies could bridge significant gaps in tax enforcement and bring informal economic activities into the fold of formal taxation.

Expanding the Tax Base: Agriculture and Professionals

Taxing agriculture and professionals poses significant challenges in developing economies. These challenges stem from the inherent characteristics of these sectors and systemic limitations in tax administration. Agriculture is often dominated by smallholder farmers who operate in dispersed, rural settings, making it difficult for tax authorities to monitor and assess their income accurately. Furthermore, many governments exempt agricultural income from taxation due to its socioeconomic and political economy significance, which creates opportunities for tax avoidance through misclassification of income. On the other hand, professionals, such as doctors, lawyers, and consultants, frequently operate in cash-heavy environments, making their earnings harder to track. Limited use of formal invoicing and weak oversight mechanisms further exacerbate tax evasion in this sector. Additionally, both sectors often resist formalization due to perceived high compliance costs and distrust of government institutions. Combined, these factors make agriculture and professionals among the hardest-to-tax sectors, contributing to significant revenue losses and highlighting the need for tailored policies to address these challenges effectively.

Taxing Agriculture Effectively

Taxing agriculture effectively in developing countries requires a combination of tailored policies, improved administrative capacity, and innovative tools to address the unique characteristics of the sector. Below are some strategies tax administrations can use to tax this sector effectively, ensuring equity and revenue generation while supporting the growth and development of the agriculture sector.

(i) **Differentiated taxation.** Implement threshold-based exemptions to protect smallholder farmers and ensure that only large-scale, commercially viable agricultural enterprises are taxed. To reduce inefficiencies caused by threshold-based taxation, design these thresholds as kinks rather than notches (Kleven and Waseem 2013). While a threshold-based exemption may introduce some complexity into the system, having some sort of exemption threshold would be optimal as the social value of administrative and compliance costs of implementing the tax on everyone may exceed the benefits of doing so, especially if the distribution of landholding is strongly skewed to the left (Keen and Mintz 2004). Introduce progressive agricultural income taxes where tax rates increase with farm size or income, ensuring equity and targeting higher-income farmers who contribute significantly to revenue potential.

(ii) **Integration with land records and property taxes.** Use land records and property valuation systems to tax agricultural holdings effectively. For instance, a land tax based on the size, location, and productivity of the land can simplify tax collection and capture agricultural income indirectly. Given that the tax would have many features of a lump-sum tax, it would also be a very efficient tax. Develop geospatial mapping and digitized land registries to improve accuracy and transparency in land-based taxation.

(iii) **Taxation through market channels.** Impose taxes at the point of agricultural output sales by collecting withholding taxes on produce sold at regulated markets, cooperatives, or through agribusiness firms. This approach minimizes the administrative burden on individual farmers. Use value-chain taxation, such as applying VAT and withholding taxes at processing and distribution points, to capture a portion of the income generated in agricultural activities. Use reverse charging, where appropriate, to shift the burden of collecting VAT on buyers rather than sellers (Buettner and Tassi 2023). Pakistan had such a policy in place for some time where the VAT liable on ginned cotton was reverse-charged to spinners, the next and more formal stage in the supply chain (Waseem 2023).

(iv) **Leveraging technology and data.** Use remote sensing and satellite imagery to assess land use, crop patterns, and productivity for accurate tax assessments. Develop digital payment systems for tax filing and collection, reducing compliance costs and increasing convenience for rural farmers (Okunogbe and Pouliquen 2022). Use smart enforcement to identify large farmers who are not paying taxes (refer to "Smart Enforcement: A Data-Driven Approach to Tax Enforcement").

(v) **Improving agricultural formalization.** Encourage the formation of farmer cooperatives and associations to bring more agricultural producers into the formal economy, making it easier to monitor and tax their activities. Provide financial and logistical incentives, such as access to subsidized credit or modern farming equipment, contingent on tax compliance.

(vi) **Eliminating exemptions and misclassification.** Close loopholes that allow nonagricultural income, such as profits from agribusiness or high-income individuals claiming agricultural exemptions, to be misclassified as agricultural income. Introduce stricter regulations and audits to ensure proper classification and limit abuse of agricultural exemptions.

(vii) **Linkage to rural development.** Make taxation part of a broader social contract, where tax revenues are reinvested in rural infrastructure, irrigation systems, and agricultural subsidies. This can help build trust among farmers and increase voluntary compliance (Luttmer and Singhal 2014).

(viii) **Capacity building for tax authorities.** Train local tax officials to better understand agricultural operations and develop specialized units for agricultural taxation. Establish mobile tax offices or rural tax outreach programs to improve accessibility and awareness among farmers (Dzansi et al. 2022).

Taxing Professionals Effectively

As mentioned, revenue authorities of developing economies struggle to tax professionals effectively. Using qualitative data on tax evasion by lawyers and dentists in Kenya, Ogembo (2019) finds that professionals do not comply with tax laws due to (i) peer influence, (ii) low levels of financial and tax capability, and (iii) the damaged political legitimacy of the tax authority. In such environments, revenue authorities can use a combination of the following strategies to ensure that professionals pay their fair share of taxes:

(i) **Mandatory digital payments and invoicing.** Enforce the use of digital payment systems for professional transactions to create an auditable trail of income. This can be achieved through incentives for professionals to adopt point-of-sale systems or mobile payment platforms. Require electronic invoicing for all transactions to improve transparency and ensure that tax authorities can track revenue flows accurately (Okunogbe and Pouliquen 2022).

(ii) **Withholding taxes at source.** Introduce withholding taxes on professional income paid by businesses, institutions, or government agencies to professionals. For example, payments for consulting, legal, or medical services can be taxed at the source. Mandate withholding on high-value professional contracts, ensuring that a portion of the tax is collected upfront (Brockmeyer and Hernandez 2021; Garriga and Tortarolo 2024).

(iii) **Taxpayer profiling and data integration.** Use big data analytics and integrate data from various sources (e.g., banks, real estate registries, licensing bodies) into a smart enforcement system. Use the system to build profiles of professionals and cross-check reported income with their lifestyles and economic activities (see "Smart Enforcement: A Data-Driven Approach to Tax Enforcement"). Develop a system of red flags to identify potential tax evasion and informality by comparing professional incomes to industry averages or peer benchmarks.

(iv) **Professional licensing and registration requirements.** Link tax compliance to the issuance or renewal of professional licenses by regulatory bodies (e.g., bar councils, medical boards). Professionals should be required to file tax returns to maintain their practice licenses. Collaborate with professional associations to ensure that their members are registered taxpayers and compliant with filing requirements.

(v) **Simplified tax regimes for small practices.** Introduce presumptive tax systems for small professional practices, where taxes are calculated based on proxies like turnover, number of clients, or office size. This reduces compliance costs while ensuring contributions from professionals operating informally. Offer standardized deductions for professional expenses to simplify the tax filing process and encourage compliance (Hoy et al. 2024).

(vi) **Incentives for formalization.** Provide tax incentives, such as reduced rates for newly registered professionals or amnesties for professionals who voluntarily disclose previously unreported income. Link tax compliance to access to government benefits, such as subsidized professional training, health insurance, or retirement schemes (Bergolo and Cruces 2021).

(vii) **Audits and targeted enforcement.** Conduct randomized or risk-based audits of professionals who consistently report low incomes compared to their peers or show unexplained wealth accumulation. Target high-income professions, such as lawyers, doctors, and architects, with industry-specific audit programs and enforcement campaigns (Best et al. 2021).

(viii) **Integration with financial institutions.** Require professionals to open designated business accounts for their transactions, enabling tax authorities to monitor cash flows and detect undeclared income. Partner with banks to report high-value deposits or transactions by professionals who are not registered taxpayers.

(ix) **Awareness and education campaigns.** Conduct outreach programs to educate professionals about their tax obligations and the benefits of compliance, emphasizing the link between tax revenue and improved public services (Ogembo 2022). Provide user-friendly tools, such as mobile apps, to help professionals calculate and file their taxes easily.

(x) **Penalties for noncompliance.** Impose significant penalties for noncompliance, such as fines, restrictions on practicing rights, or public naming and shaming for professionals evading taxes (Slemrod et al. 2022; Dwenger and Treber 2022). Ensure enforcement is fair and consistent to build trust and deter tax evasion (Luttmer and Singhal 2014).

By implementing these strategies, governments can effectively address underreporting and noncompliance among professionals, ensuring equitable contributions to tax revenue while fostering a transparent and fair tax system.

Informality and Tax Rates

Can lower tax rates induce firms to formalize? The relationship between informality and tax rates is complex. High tax rates can incentivize businesses to remain informal to avoid tax burdens, while lower tax rates may encourage formalization by reducing the cost of compliance. However, the effectiveness of tax rate reductions in promoting formalization depends on various factors, including enforcement mechanisms, administrative capacity, and the broader regulatory environment.

Empirical evidence supporting the notion that lower tax rates can encourage formalization is mixed. Rocha et al. (2018) use the SIMPLES program from Brazil to show that reducing taxes once registration costs have already been eliminated reduces firm informality.[5] This effect comes from the formalization of existing informal firms, and not from the creation of new formal businesses nor greater formal firm survival. The implied formalization elasticity, however, is low, meaning that the program resulted in net losses for the country in terms of tax revenues. Using the same program, Monteiro and Assuncao (2012) find heterogeneous effects by sectors. While formal licensing goes up by 13 percentage points in the retail sector, it remains unchanged in the construction, transportation, services, and manufacturing sectors (see Fajnzylber et al. 2011 for other impacts of the program).

While lower tax rates may not encourage formalization of firms, increasing the tax rate significantly can push registered firms into informality. Waseem (2018) uses a tax reform enacted by Pakistan in 2009, which increased the taxation of partnership earnings substantially relative to earnings from other business forms, to show that following the tax increase nearly two-thirds of the affected firms moved into informality. The revenue loss caused by this migration was so large that by the third year after the tax increase the government was collecting less revenue than it would have without the tax increase.

The complex relationship between informality and tax rates underscores the need for policymakers to exercise caution when designing tax policies aimed at addressing informality. While lowering tax rates may incentivize formalization, it may also lead to revenue losses if not paired with effective enforcement and broadening of the tax base. Conversely, significantly increasing tax rates to enhance revenue risks pushing formal firms into informality, as evidenced by studies showing that higher tax burdens often incentivize firms to evade taxes by exiting the formal sector. This delicate balance requires policymakers to carefully evaluate the trade-offs and complement tax rate adjustments with measures such as simplified compliance procedures, targeted enforcement, and support for businesses transitioning to formal operations. A nuanced approach, informed by empirical evidence, is crucial to ensure that tax policies effectively reduce informality without undermining revenue goals or economic activity.

---

5 The SIMPLES program in Brazil, introduced in 1996, is a simplified tax regime designed to encourage small and micro enterprises to formalize by consolidating multiple taxes into a single, lower tax rate and streamlining compliance procedures. By reducing the administrative burden and cost of formalization, the program aimed to increase formal registrations among small businesses while improving tax compliance.

CHAPTER 4

Case Studies

This section examines the efforts of three ADB developing member countries to expand their tax base and address the challenges of taxing informal and HTT sectors. By analyzing the strategies, successes, and limitations of these individual cases, broader policy lessons and practical insights can be derived to assist governments in other contexts in designing effective and sustainable tax reforms. These case studies provide a nuanced understanding of how tailored approaches can help overcome the unique obstacles faced by developing economies.

Pakistan: Tax Base Expands But Not Revenue

This case study explores Pakistan's efforts to expand its tax base by enhancing compliance and formalizing its extensive informal sector. Despite numerous reforms, Pakistan's tax-to-GDP ratio remains below regional averages, hindered by the limited reach of its tax system and the widespread prevalence of informal economic activity.

Pakistan's Income Tax System: Key Trends

Nominal income tax revenue is increasing but there is no growth in real terms. Figure 13 displays Pakistan's income tax revenue from 2007 to 2021, measured both in nominal terms (in Pakistan rupees, represented by green bars) and in real terms, as a percentage of GDP (shown by the blue line). The green bars show a steady increase in nominal income tax revenue, rising from under PRs500 billion in 2007 to nearly PRs1,500 billion in 2021. This upward trend may convince policymakers and the public that reforms aimed at expanding the tax base and improving compliance are working. However, in real terms, tax revenue as a share of GDP has remained stagnant, fluctuating 3%–4% for most of the period. This discrepancy suggests that while more revenue is being collected, little progress has been made in enhancing compliance or effectively capturing income from informal and HTT sectors.

Tax base is expanding from a narrow base. Figure 14 illustrates the trend in the number of tax filers in Pakistan from 2007 to 2021. While the total number of tax filers (green bars) has generally increased over the period, a substantial portion of the tax filers each year consists of individuals reporting zero tax payment (red segment of the bars). This highlights a key challenge in expanding the tax base. When revenue authorities focus too much attention on individuals and businesses that fail to file tax returns, a common response is for these taxpayers to register as filers but declare no or minimal taxable income. Noncompliance within the registered sector is a central theme of this report, underscoring that simply increasing the number of filers is unlikely to expand the fiscal capacity of the state.

Figure 13: Pakistan's Income Tax Revenue, 2007–2021

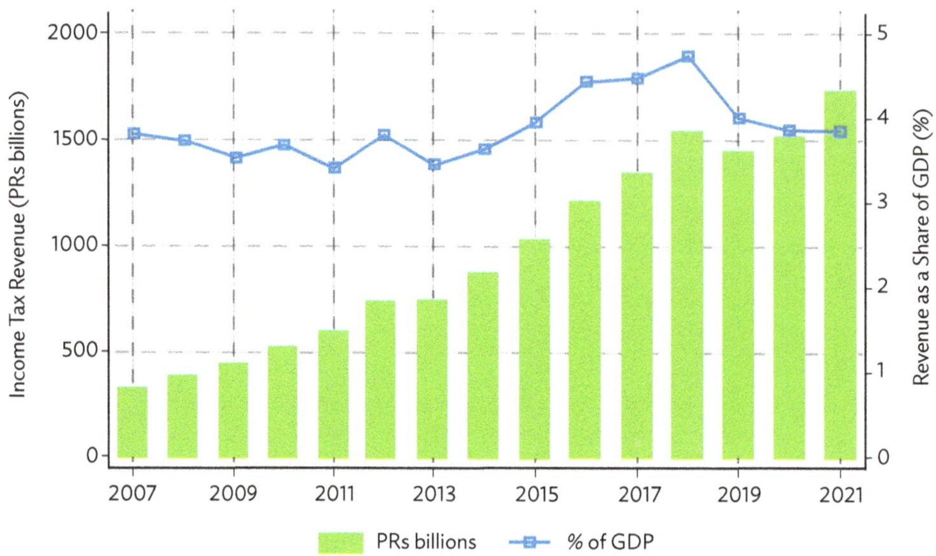

GDP = gross domestic product, PR = Pakistan rupee.
Source: Government of Pakistan, Federal Board of Revenue. FBR Year Books 2007–2021 (accessed 11 November 2024).

Figure 14: Number of Income Tax Filers in Pakistan, 2007–2021

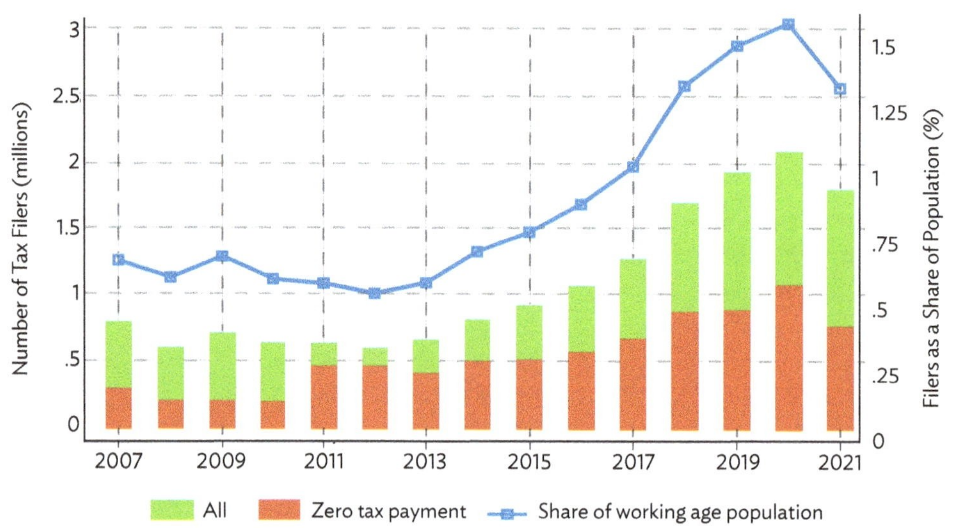

Sources: Federal Board of Revenue. FBR Year Books 2007–2021 and FBR Taxpayer Directory (accessed 11 November 2024).

Tax revenue is concentrated at the top. Figure 15A illustrates the share of total income tax paid by the top 0.1%, 1%, 10%, and 25% of taxpayers in Pakistan from 2007 to 2021. Over this period, there is persistently high concentration of tax contributions among the top 0.1% and 1% of earners, with these groups contributing most income tax revenue. The trends underscore the narrow tax base in Pakistan, where a small fraction of high-income earners shoulder most of the income tax burden. Figure 15B reinforces this message, illustrating that tax payments remain low across most income percentiles, with significant contributions only at the top. This skewed distribution reflects a high dependency on the top earners for tax revenue and suggests that the bulk of taxpayers contribute minimally, if at all, to total income tax collections.

Figure 15: Pakistan's Concentration of Income Tax Revenue at the Top, 2007–2021

A: Contributions of Top Earners

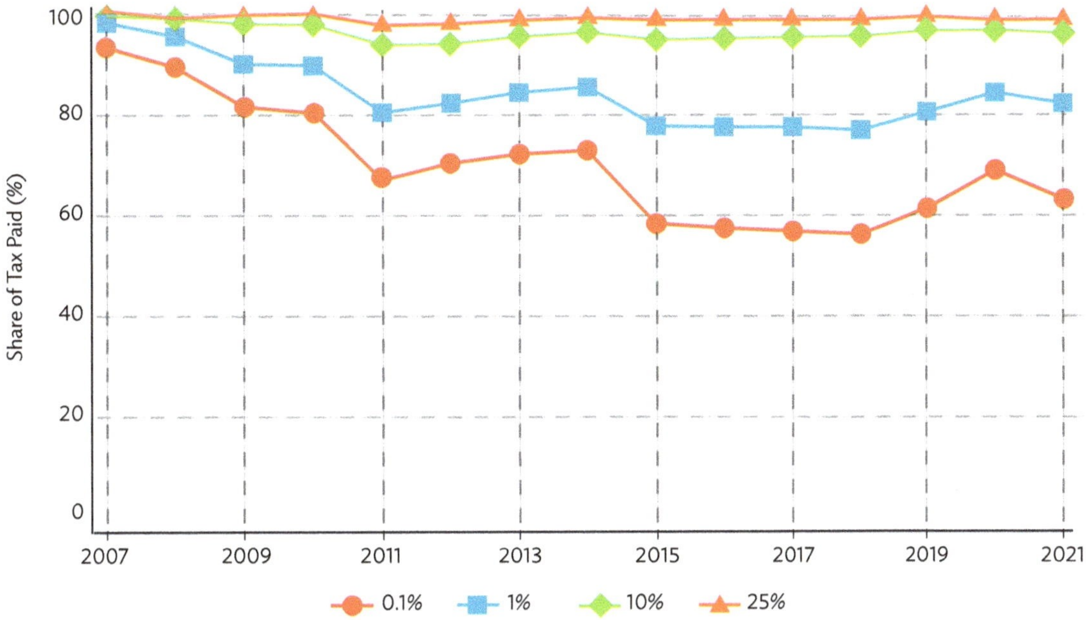

B: Tax Revenue by Percentiles

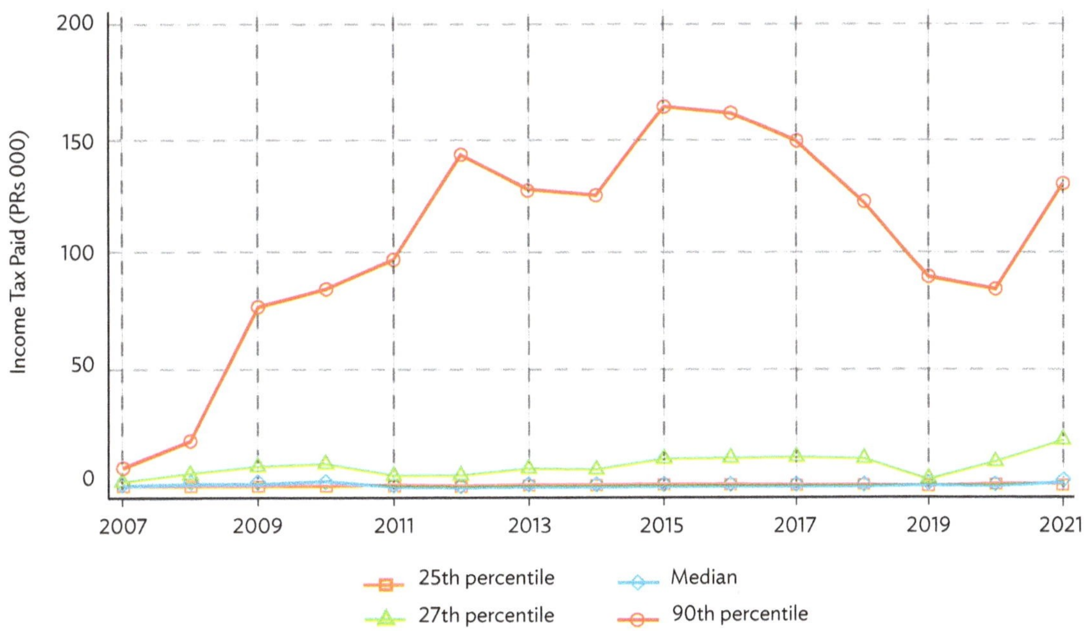

Source: Z. Farooq, O. Ur Rehman, and M. Waseem. 2024. Predistribution Vs. Redistribution: The Role of Taxes, Transfers, and Public Spending in Reducing Inequality. Working Paper. Unpublished.

Growth in filers outpaces revenue growth, with new taxpayers contributing trivial amounts to total revenue. Figure 16B compares the growth of tax filers and income tax revenue from them relative to their levels in 2007. The red line represents the growth in the number of filers, which has accelerated significantly since 2014, reaching over three times the 2007 level by 2019. In contrast, income tax revenue growth, shown by the blue line, has been largely absent, with the country essentially collecting the same amount of income tax in real terms in 2021 as in 2007. Figure16A breaks down total income tax revenue by existing versus new taxpayers from 2008 to 2021. The data reveal that existing taxpayers consistently account for almost all income tax revenue, with contributions from new taxpayers remaining minimal across the entire period.

Figure 16: Base Broadening Versus Base Deepening in Pakistan, 2007–2021

A: Contributions of New Taxpayers

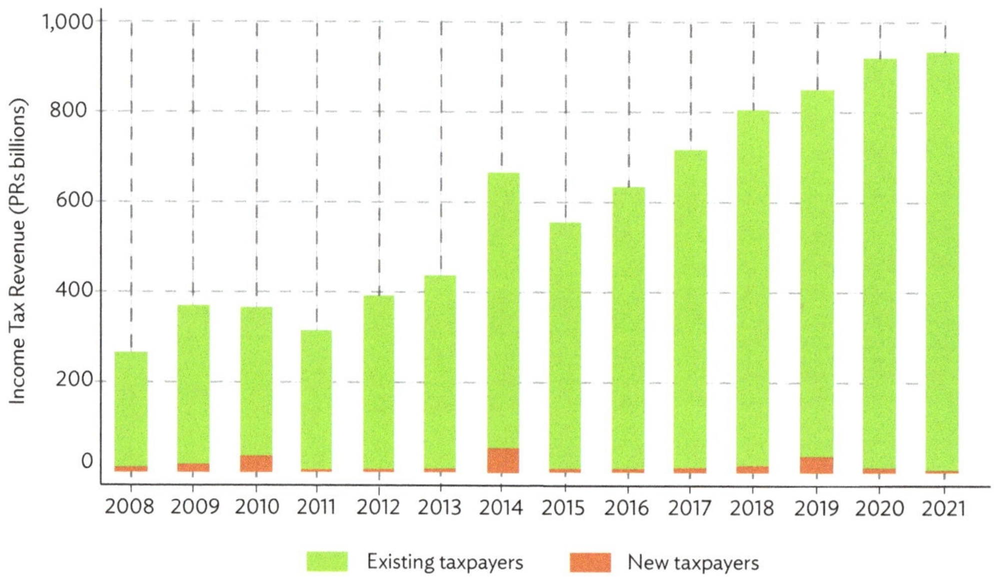

B: Filers Growth Versus Revenue Growth

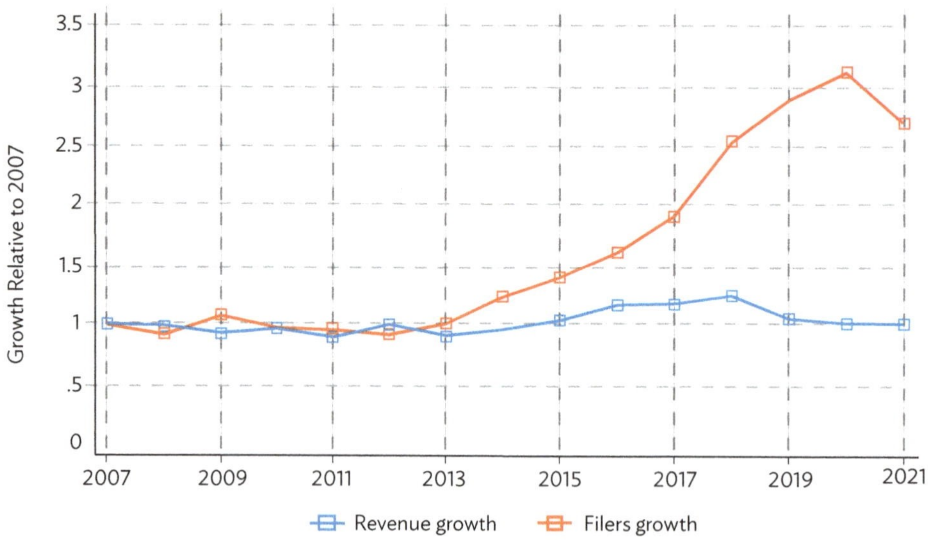

Source: Z. Farooq, O. Ur Rehman, and M. Waseem. 2024. Predistribution Vs. Redistribution: The Role of Taxes, Transfers, and Public Spending in Reducing Inequality. Working Paper. Unpublished.

Figure 17: Informality in Pakistan, 2006–2022

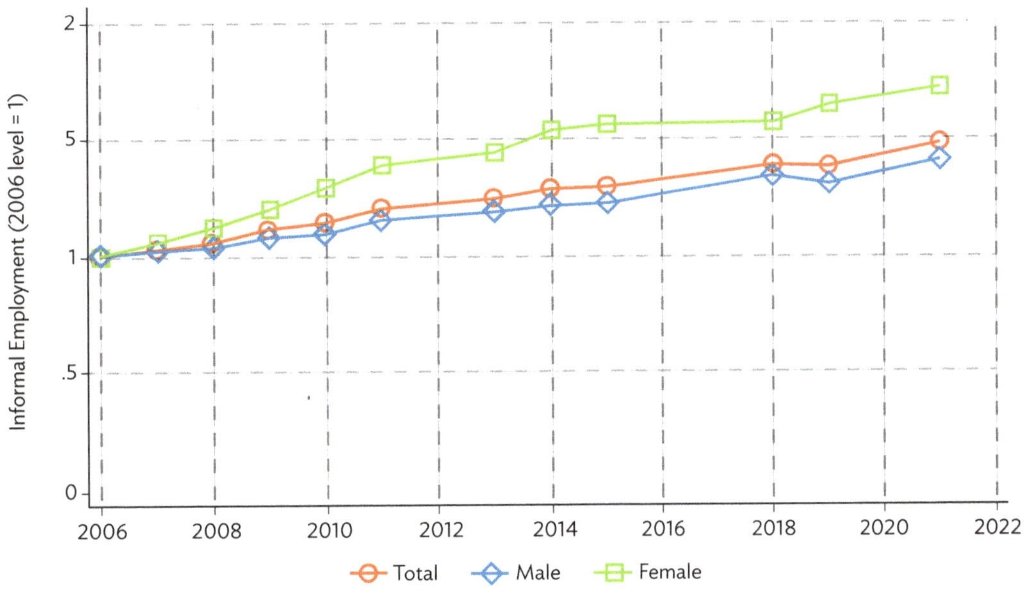

Source: International Labour Organization (accessed 11 November 2024).

Informality in Pakistan

How has informality evolved in Pakistan? Figure 17 explores this question using ILO data. Informal employment—disaggregated by total, male, and female informal employment—is normalized to 2006 levels, setting it at 1 so that subsequent levels capture changes relative to 2006. Over the years, informal employment shows a steady upward trajectory, reflecting the persistence of informality within the labor market. Notably, female informal employment has risen significantly compared to male informal employment and overall informal employment. This trend underscores the entrenched nature of informality in Pakistan, with gender disparities pointing to the need for targeted policies to enhance formal sector participation, particularly for women. Pakistan's case also makes an interesting comparison with Viet Nam, where informal employment, especially female informal employment, has shrunk sharply since 2013.

Pakistan's Costly Efforts to Expand Its Tax Base

In recent years, Pakistan has implemented a range of intrusive, costly measures to broaden its tax base. These measures are aimed at increasing the costs of operating outside the registered tax regime by penalizing nonfiling. These measures include:

(i) **Higher withholding tax rates on nonfilers.** A distinction between tax filers and nonfilers, leading to differential withholding tax rates, was introduced through the Finance Act of 2014. This legislation marked the first instance where nonfilers were subjected to higher withholding tax rates compared to filers. The primary objective of this policy was to incentivize tax compliance by imposing higher tax rates on individuals and entities that did not file their income tax returns. Over the years, the government has continued to adjust these rates and has introduced new categories for additional withholding.

Table 8: Pakistan's Withholding Tax Rates on Filers Versus Nonfilers

Item	Withholding Tax Rate (%)	
	Filers	Nonfilers
Imports	6	12
Dividends	15	30
Profit on debt	15	35
Payments to nonresident persons	5.5	11
Payments for goods, services, and contracts	5	10
Rent of immovable property	0–25	0–50
Prizes and winnings	20	40
Sale of petroleum products	12	24
Cash withdrawal	0	0.6
Purchase of motor vehicles	1.5–36	3–72
Brokerage and commission	12	24
Transfer of immovable property	3	6
Sales to distributors and wholesalers	0.1	2
Sales to retailers	0.5	2.5
Purchase of immovable property	3	6
Amount remitted abroad through credit or debit cards	5	10

Source: Government of Pakistan, Federal Board of Revenue. 2024. Withholding Tax Regime (Rates Card).

Table 8 provides a list of some of these withholding taxes. Tax rates on filers and nonfilers are distinguished from each other, and where more than one rate is applicable to a category, only the most typical rate is listed.[6] In general, the withholding tax rate applicable to nonfilers is twice that of filers. In some cases, however, this rate is substantially higher (e.g., 20 times for sales to distributors and wholesalers).

(i) **Restrictions on engaging in high-value transactions.** To further discourage noncompliance, the government has imposed outright restrictions on nonfilers to buy property and engage in other transactions. Since 2018, nonfilers have been prohibited from purchasing properties valued above PRs5 million. Additionally, these restrictions apply to the transfer of property ownership, requiring both buyers and sellers to be registered taxpayers for transactions above the specified threshold. In addition to property restrictions, Pakistan has implemented bans on vehicle purchases and registration for nonfilers.

[6] For the complete list of withholding taxes, see Government of Pakistan, Federal Board of Revenue. 2024. Withholding Tax Regime (Rates Card).

(ii) **Mandatory proof of tax filing for professional licenses and contracts.** To enforce compliance within the professional sector, the government has mandated that individuals provide proof of tax filing when applying for certain professional licenses and government contracts. For example, consultants, contractors, and suppliers who wish to work with government entities must be registered tax filers, a requirement intended to formalize freelance and contractual work, which is often part of the informal economy. Additionally, certain professional bodies, such as bar councils, now require their members to be registered taxpayers.

Measures against nonfiling are becoming increasingly stringent over time. New proposals currently being contemplated include:

- **Foreign travel ban.** Nonfilers will be prohibited from undertaking international travel. Exceptions will include travel for religious or educational purposes.
- **Cash withdrawal limit.** A proposed annual cash withdrawal limit of PRs30 million will be imposed on nonfilers.
- **Asset purchase restrictions.** Nonfilers will be barred from purchasing immovable properties and vehicles.
- **Investment limitations.** Investments in the stock market and mutual funds will be restricted for nonfilers.
- **Banking constraints.** Nonfilers will face restrictions on opening current bank accounts.
- **Increased scrutiny.** Nonfilers will be subject to enhanced audits and scrutiny by tax authorities.

Are These Measures Working?

Despite Pakistan's aggressive measures to expand its tax base, the evidence suggests that these efforts have had little or no impact on revenue generation. Figure 16, for example, shows that while the number of registered tax filers in the country has increased significantly in recent years, reaching over three times the 2007 level by 2019, with major growth coming after 2014 when these aggressive measures against nonfiling were introduced, the income tax revenue as a percentage of GDP has remained stagnant, fluctuating 3%–4% over the past decade. This lack of growth in real revenue indicates that new tax filers are contributing little to overall tax collections, raising questions about the effectiveness of these costly compliance measures. Simply adding more names to the list of registered taxpayers has not translated into meaningful revenue gains, suggesting that many new filers report minimal or zero taxable income. Consequently, despite the higher withholding taxes, transactional restrictions, and other compliance requirements, these measures appear to have created more administrative burden than tangible revenue outcomes.

Beyond revenue generation, it is unclear if there are any substantial nonrevenue benefits from expanding the tax base. It is well known in literature that the direct benefits of taxing the informal sector are likely to be relatively modest, and the implications for vertical equity potentially adverse (see "What Is the Revenue

Potential of the Informal Sector?"). The weight of the argument for taxing the informal sector thus turns on indirect benefits, notably the prospect of accelerated growth and the potential for governance and equity gains (Joshi et al. 2014). For example, taxation of small informal firms may ensure higher tax compliance in future if they expand over time. Doing so could thus foster a culture of tax compliance. In a related argument, bringing informal firms into the tax net is argued to promote equity, suggesting that the failure of informal firms to pay taxes can be viewed by formal firms as being unfair. This can lower general tax morale and discourage tax compliance among larger firms (Alm et al. 2005). While both these claims are intuitive, evidence remains highly imperfect. It is widely believed that taxing small firms can build a culture of tax compliance, but there is no systematic evidence on the long-term impact of small business taxation on attitudes toward taxation among those firms. Meanwhile, evidence that informality can lead to reduced tax morale is limited to cross-country correlations, with corresponding difficulties in asserting causation (Joshi et al. 2014). There is no available evidence from Pakistan to suggest that these benefits are materializing on a large scale.

Another indirect benefit of increased filing is the availability of more and better data. To the extent that these additional data help informed decision-making, they may stimulate revenue collection in other ways, such as through improved targeting of tax audits. But note that measures to increase filings have now been in place for nearly 10 years. If additional data generated by these measures were helpful, these effects would now be visible in revenue collection, but no such effect is found.

Whether these aggressive measures to expand the tax base in Pakistan are successful ultimately depends on the government's objective. Under the standard welfare analysis, these measures would be considered effective if the social value of revenue and nonrevenue benefits from expanded tax filing outweigh the social value of compliance and administrative costs they impose (Keen and Mintz 2004). However, with clear evidence showing that the increase in registered filers has not translated into meaningful revenue gains and no substantial evidence of nonrevenue benefits, such as improved economic formalization or enhanced financial transparency, these policies appear suboptimal from a policy perspective. These measures impose compliance costs on taxpayers, administrative costs on the government, and hurt economic activity. The absence of measurable benefits against the backdrop of these significant costs suggests that the current approach may need reevaluation to better align with sustainable fiscal objectives.

Policy Lessons

Pakistan offers valuable lessons for policymakers in DMCs aiming to expand their tax base and formalize the informal sector. A key takeaway is that aggressive measures to increase tax filings do not necessarily lead to higher revenue collections or broader economic benefits. To this extent, Pakistan's experience is consistent with that of Rwanda, South Africa, Uganda, and other economies mentioned in the "Expanding Business Registration" section, where an expanded tax base did not result in higher revenue (Lediga et al. 2025; Jouste et al. 2021; Mascagni et al. 2022). In Pakistan's case, these policies expanded the tax base nominally but failed to generate significant revenue gains, as many new filers either reported minimal income or remained noncompliant in their actual tax contributions.

Policymakers should consider that simply increasing the number of registered taxpayers does not equate to a more robust tax system. Instead, they may need to focus on targeted approaches that enhance compliance among existing taxpayers while simplifying the tax process to encourage genuine participation. Revenue authorities operate with limited enforcement resources, necessitating strategic decisions about where to allocate these efforts for the greatest impact.
Whether resources should be directed toward expanding the tax base by adding new filers or enhancing compliance among existing taxpayers depends on the returns to effort in each of these areas. Pakistan's experience shows that focusing solely on expanding the tax base without ensuring meaningful compliance among existing taxpayers yields minimal revenue gains and increases administrative costs. For policymakers in DMCs, it is essential to gather systematic evidence on how returns on investment differ between expanding the tax base and improving compliance. This data-driven approach would allow authorities to allocate resources more effectively, maximizing revenue potential while minimizing unnecessary burdens. Without a clear understanding of where enforcement efforts are most productive, blindly pursuing tax base expansion is unlikely to achieve sustainable fiscal outcomes. Additionally, careful assessment of the potential nonrevenue benefits, such as economic formalization or improved data on economic activity, is essential. Expanding the tax base should be pursued only if these benefits clearly outweigh the compliance costs for taxpayers and the administrative burden on the government, ensuring a balanced approach that fosters long-term fiscal sustainability.

Viet Nam: Successful Reforms to Reduce Informality?

Among the focus countries, Viet Nam seems to have made the most notable strides in taxing informal and HTT sectors. This progress occurred following several measures the government implemented to broaden the tax base and enhance compliance (see Shukla et al. 2011 and Thanh et al. 2014 for details). These measures can be divided into three areas:

(i) **Tax system reforms.** Viet Nam undertook comprehensive tax reforms aimed at modernizing its tax administration and expanding the tax base. These reforms include simplifying tax procedures, reducing tax rates, and broadening the taxpayer base to capture income from the informal sector.

(ii) **VAT adjustments.** The government made efforts to expand the VAT base by reducing exemptions and preferential treatments. By broadening the scope of VAT, the policy aimed to include more businesses from the informal sector, encouraging them to formalize their operations to comply with tax obligations.

(iii) **Enhancement of tax administration**. Viet Nam invested in modernizing its tax administration through digitalization and improved data management. This included the development of electronic tax filing systems and the integration of tax data across agencies to better track economic activities, making it more difficult for informal businesses to evade taxes.

New Legislation to Reform the Income Tax System

In this case study, the focus is on the introduction of new income tax legislation in 2009, to study its impacts on informality and other outcomes. In 2009, Viet Nam introduced comprehensive income tax legislation aimed at increasing tax compliance, broadening its tax base, and improving revenue collection. By modernizing the tax system, the government sought to capture income from previously untaxed sectors, reduce reliance on corporate income tax, and create a more balanced revenue stream from both individual and business taxpayers. Key provisions of the 2009 income tax legislation were:

(i) **Lowering personal income tax rates.** The government reduced PIT rates to encourage voluntary compliance and reduce the tax burden on small businesses. By making the tax system more equitable, the aim was to encourage a larger portion of the population to file taxes and discourage informal income reporting.

(ii) **Broadening the tax base.** The legislation included measures to expand the tax base by introducing taxes on different income sources, including wages, dividends, and capital gains. This change was intended to capture more diverse sources of income, particularly from individuals and small businesses operating in the informal sector.

(iii) **Strengthening tax administration.** The law introduced stricter penalties for noncompliance, reinforced audit practices, and improved tax collection processes. The Viet Nam General Department of Taxation implemented these changes to reduce tax evasion and encourage compliance.

How Has the New Legislation Impacted Informality in Viet Nam?

Figure 18 examines the evolution of informality in the country from 2007 to 2023. Data on informal employment by gender from the ILO are used and plotted for these years, normalizing the level of informal employment of each type in 2009—the baseline year—at one. Three clear trends are visible in this plot:

(i) The 2009 legislation did not immediately cause a reduction in informality. In fact, informality continued to rise until 2013, 4 years after the introduction of the new legislation.

(ii) A clear downward trend in informality began in 2013 and continued until 2020.

(iii) Informal employment among females declined at a faster rate compared to males, with female informal employment dropping to around less than 80% of its 2009 level in 2020. In comparison, male informal employment did not decrease during these years. This gender-specific shift in employment dynamics suggests that the structural transformation Viet Nam experienced in the 2010s was more concentrated on sectors with heavy female employment, like domestic work, hospitality, and retail. Worsening of female informal employment since 2020 indicates that the coronavirus disease pandemic has likely affected these sectors disproportionately.

Overall, the figure highlights Viet Nam's progress in reducing informal employment over the last decade. At a broad level, it signals the effectiveness of policy interventions aimed at formalizing the economy. But it is difficult to attribute all this progress to policy measures alone as Viet Nam's economy grew rapidly during this period. With growth, the benefits of operating in the formal sector rise as the firm could use superior production technology, serve a bigger market, and hire more productive formal workers (Kleven et al. 2016). This would accelerate the organic movement of firms from informal to formal sectors.

Figure 18B plots the GDP growth rate of Viet Nam from 2007 to 2023. Comparing both panels of the figure shows that GDP growth accelerates exactly from the year 2013, when informal employment starts to go down, and the sharp drop in growth in 2020 is also reflected in total and female informal employment going up. These macroeconomic effects would also have contributed to the reduction in informality seen from 2013 onward. But regardless of its source, the progress made by Viet Nam to reduce informality is impressive relative to other developing economies in the region. In Pakistan, for example, during a similar period, informal employment went up by nearly 50%.

Figure 18: Informality and GDP Growth in Viet Nam, 2007–2023

A: Informal Employment by Gender

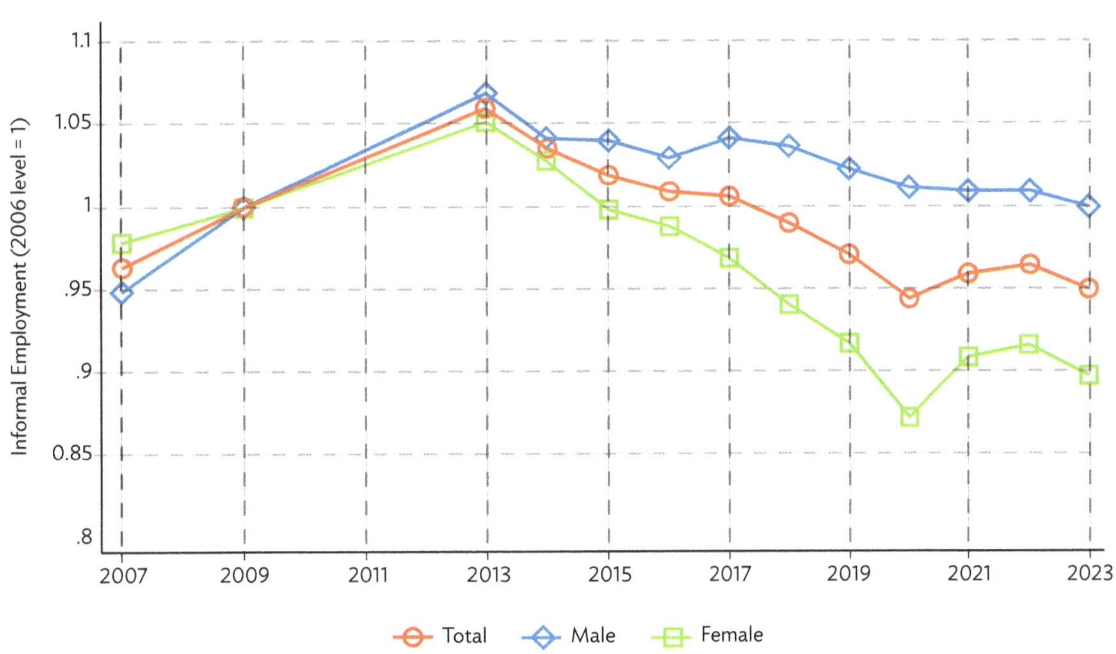

B: GDP Growth Rate

GDP = gross domestic product.

Source: International Labour Organization and World Bank. World Development Indicators (accessed 11 November 2024).

Figure 19 uses data from the World Bank Enterprise Survey to observe trends in the formalization of firms and their interactions with the revenue authority in Viet Nam. First, two measures of firm formalization are examined. The top bars show that the proportion of firms registered when they began operations slightly increases over time, although data for only 2 years are available. This trend, however, is clearer in the next measure, which shows the average number of years between a business starting operations and formally registering. This time lag has reduced sharply during our sample period. The average number of years between a business starting operations and formally registering peaked in 2009, reaching nearly 6 years. By 2023, this lag has reduced significantly, suggesting that among other things the government must have made it easier and faster for businesses to register.

Figure 19: Evolution of Informality in Viet Nam

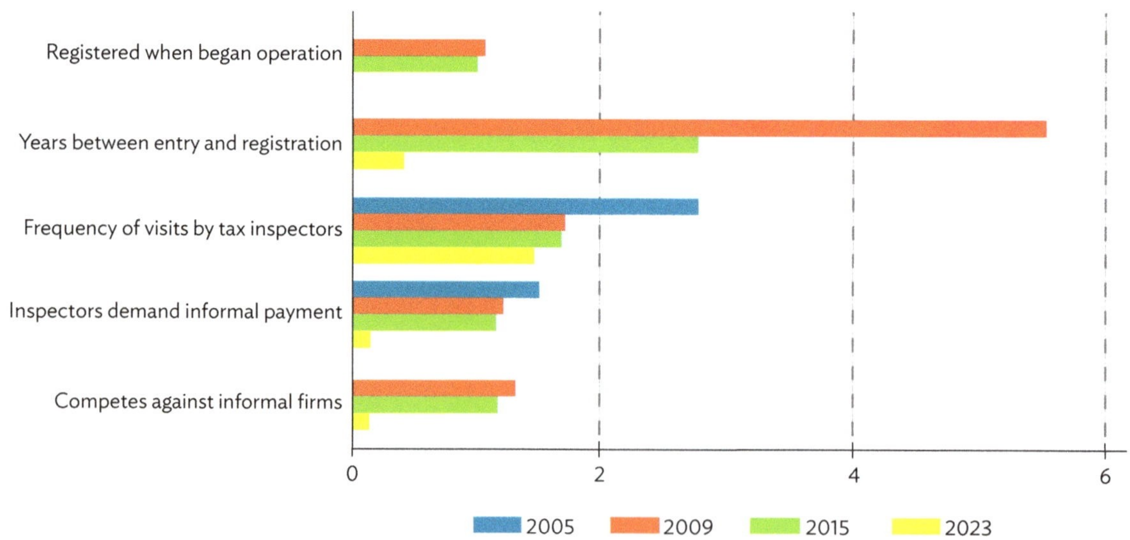

Source: World Bank. Enterprise Surveys Data (accessed 11 November 2024).

Three measures of the tax, regulatory, and competitive environments in which Vietnamese firms operate are examined.

(i) **Frequency of tax inspections.** The average frequency of tax inspections declined significantly between 2005 and 2009 and has been relatively stable since. This trend implies that while the government has maintained enforcement efforts, inspections perhaps are more targeted, particularly with the adoption of digital tools in recent years.

(ii) **Incidence of informal payments.** The proportion of businesses reporting tax inspectors demanding informal payments has declined over time, especially between 2015 and 2023. The significant reduction indicates progress in reducing corruption, which in turn will help building trust and transparency in tax administration.

(iii) **Competition with informal firms**. The extent to which formal businesses perceive competition from informal firms has declined steadily since 2009. This trend suggests that efforts to formalize businesses and level the playing field have been partially effective, reducing the advantages that informal firms previously enjoyed by avoiding taxes and regulatory compliance.

This analysis further highlights the great progress Viet Nam has made to formalize businesses and improve tax administration. On all measures for which data are available, remarkable progress over time, especially after 2015, has occurred. These findings reinforce the importance of sustaining policy efforts to simplify registration processes, enhance transparency, and support businesses in transitioning to formality.

Obstacles to Growing Businesses

The World Bank Enterprise Survey asks respondents to assess major obstacles to their firm's growth and performance on a scale of 1–10. Figure 20 highlights the evolution of key obstacles faced by firms in Viet Nam, as identified in the survey. Each obstacle is measured by its mean value on a standardized scale, with higher values indicating greater perceived challenges. Key insights from this analysis include:

(i) **Practices of the informal sector.** This remains a persistent obstacle throughout the years, with consistently high and increasing values indicating that competition from informal enterprises continues to place pressure on formal businesses. Figure 19 shows that over time fewer Vietnamese firms are reporting that they face competition from informal firms. When read together with the obstacles data, it shows that competition from the informal sector is becoming less of a concern in many sectors but where it persists registered firms perhaps feel it to be the biggest obstacle in running and growing their businesses.

(ii) **Tax rates and administration.** Tax rates and administration were major concerns in 2005, reflecting a challenging business environment for formal enterprises. Over time, the perceived burden of tax administration has noticeably declined, especially in 2009, likely due to the new income tax law Viet Nam introduced to modernize its tax system and expand its tax base. However, tax rates remain a moderate concern, highlighting ongoing dissatisfaction with the cost of compliance.

(iii) **Corruption.** Corruption was a substantial obstacle in 2005 but has shown steady improvement over the years, reflecting Viet Nam's efforts to reduce informal payments and promote transparency in its administrative processes. This is consistent with the previous figure, which uses a different metric.

(iv) **Business licensing and permits.** This area shows significant progress over time, with a marked decline in the mean value by 2023, indicating that reforms aimed at simplifying licensing processes and reducing compliance costs have been effective in reducing regulatory burdens for businesses.

(v) **Labor regulations.** Perceptions of labor regulations as an obstacle have decreased over the years, particularly from 2005 to 2009. This decline suggests further reductions in compliance costs, although the issue remained relatively stable from 2015 to 2023, signaling room for further refinement.

(vi) **Access to finance.** This was the most significant challenge in 2005, with the highest mean value among all obstacles. By 2023, this improved substantially, reflecting better financial inclusion and increased availability of credit for businesses.

Figure 20: Obstacles to Conducting Business in Viet Nam

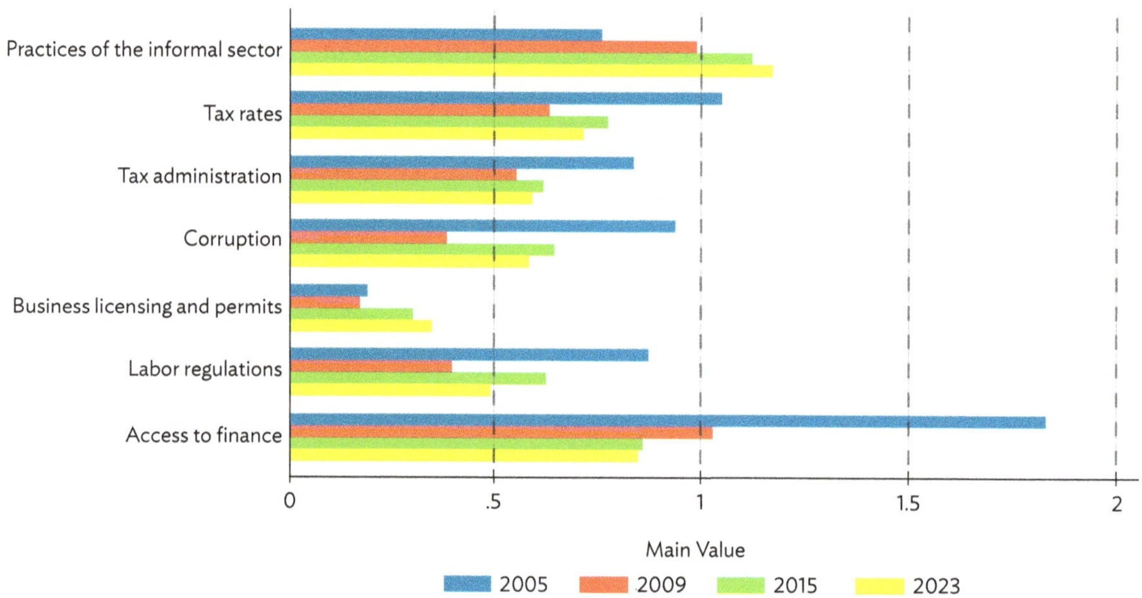

Source: Author's calculations using data from World Bank. Enterprise Surveys Data (accessed 11 November 2024).

Overall, our case study highlights Viet Nam's steady progress in addressing several structural and administrative barriers faced by businesses, particularly in the areas of tax administration, corruption, licensing, and access to finance. Viet Nam's case can thus be a template for other DMCs to introduce meaningful reforms to reduce informality, enhance fairness, and further ease regulatory and financial constraints for formal businesses.

India: The Tax Base and Introduction of the Goods and Services Tax

In 2017, India replaced a multitude of taxes on goods and services at the national and subnational level with a nationwide goods and services tax (GST). The GST was a fundamental reform that has had many far-reaching consequences, including on expanding the tax base.

The government's economic survey of 2017–2018 estimated that the introduction of the GST resulted in a 50% increase in the number of registered taxpayers from about 6.4 million to 9.8 million (Government of India, Ministry of Finance 2018). About 1.7 million of these GST registrations were by taxpayers whose turnover was below the mandatory registration threshold, showing the strong incentive to register voluntarily under the GST.

Prior to the GST, Indian states had subnational VATs, which themselves improved the revenue performance of Indian states. However, VAT credits would not carry over across states. In addition, there was a turnover tax on cross-state transactions, and a host of entry taxes on cross-border movement of goods. At the central level, there was a VAT on manufactured goods known as the CenVAT. The GST therefore represented a substantial reduction in the complexity of taxes especially for entities engaged in cross-border trade, whether directly or indirectly, through their supply chain (Barnwal et al. 2024). It raised the value of registration because of the availability of tax credits on input taxes.

However, as is the case with VAT systems (and other tax instruments) worldwide, most revenue is concentrated at the very largest firms. As Figure 21 shows, the top 1% of firms by turnover account for 50% of total net GST collection. The bottom 50% of firms together account for less than 1% of total GST collection. These are striking statistics that suggest that the revenue gains from the GST do not come from formalization of small, informal firms.

Figure 21: Distribution of Tax Revenue Across Percentile of Firm Turnover in India

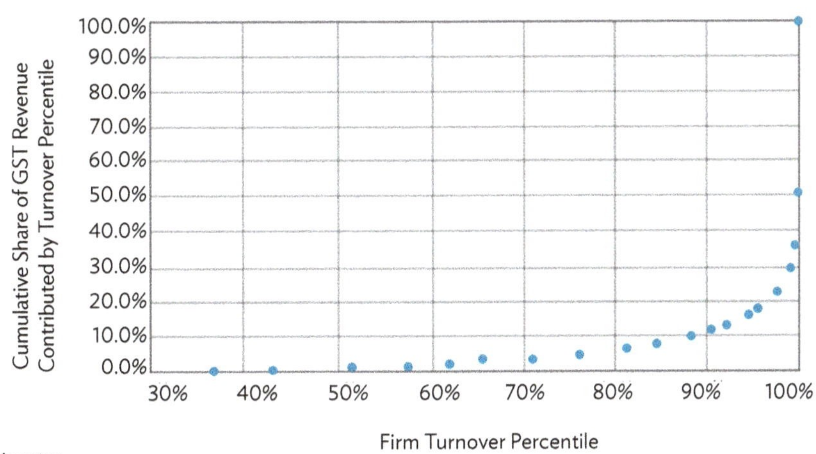

GST = goods and services tax.

Note: Figure shows the cumulative contribution to net GST revenue from taxpayers across the firm turnover size distribution. The top 1% largest firms account for 50% of net GST revenue.

Source: Authors' calculations using data from Government of India, Ministry of Finance. GST Statistics (accessed 14 January 2025).

The GST has substantially improved the government's enforcement capacity through digitalization. All tax returns are e-filed, permitting automatic cross-checks of information. For example, the government requires e-way bills for the movement of goods above a certain monetary threshold. It then links the ability to generate e-way bills to compliance along other margins such as the filing and payment of GST liabilities. Similarly, it links credit provision to filing and payment of the GST.

Overall, as Figure 22 shows, formality has increased in India since the GST. Between 2014 and 2022, firms became less likely to see competing against informal firms as a barrier to growth, and firms operate for fewer years as an informal firm. Administration, as proxied by visits from the tax authority, has improved. However, there has been a large increase in firms perceiving tax administration as a barrier to growth, from about 14% to 23%. This increase seems to be largest in sectors such as information technology and construction, where the GST introduction has been the most transformative, but is seen across most sectors (Figure 23). This increase reflects the fact that the success of enforcement in the GST has often relied in electronic methods that reduce flexibility for the taxpayer. For example, taxpayers are automatically barred from generating e-way bills or filing their GST credit provision form if they have not made any GST payment. Their GST credits are automatically limited to the credits that their suppliers have filed. There have been several legal challenges to these rules that increasingly place the enforcement burden on the taxpayer.

Figure 22: Change in Informality and Compliance Costs in India After Goods and Service Tax Introduction in 2017

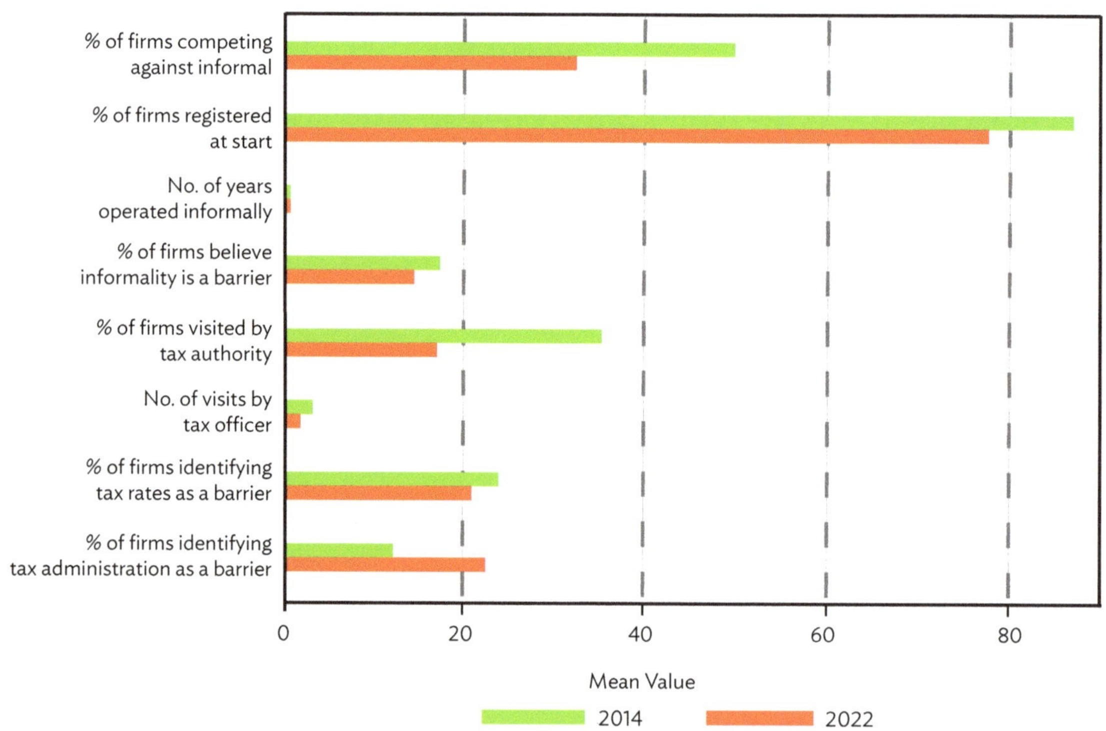

Source: Author's calculations using data from World Bank. Enterprise Surves Data (accessed 11 November 2024).

Figure 23: Increase in Compliance Costs Across Industries, 2014–2022

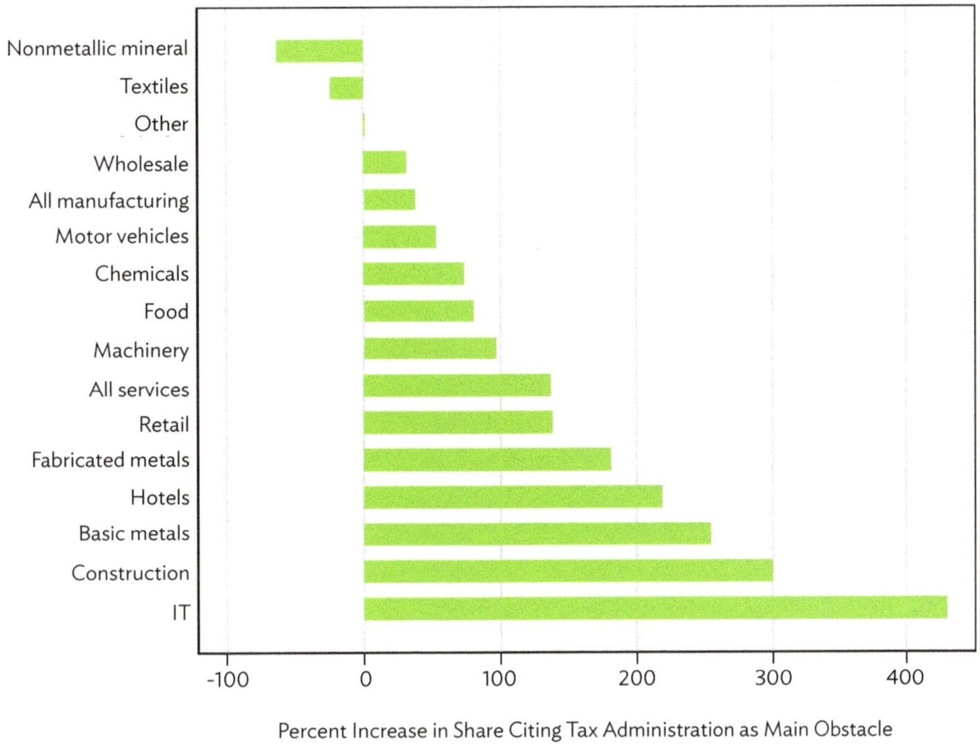

Source: Author's calculations using data from World Bank. Enterprise Surveys Data (accessed 11 November 2024).

India's experience with the GST is emblematic of the interaction between VAT and informality described in the section "Value-Added Tax and Informality." It has increased the benefits of formalization while reducing costs for most sectors, thereby encouraging registration. At the same time, the bulk of revenue is generated by the top of the firm distribution, and any benefits to increased formalization among small firms are primarily nonrevenue benefits in terms of morale or generation of statistics on economic activity. A clean register is of crucial importance to curtail loss of revenue through overclaiming of input tax credits. The issue of deregistering bogus firms is of increasing policy relevance and experimentation (Mahajan et al. 2024). Revenue authorities have engaged in drives to identify and remove thousands of bogus firms each year (Government of India 2024). The GST has shifted the policy focus from increasing registrations to maintaining a clean and active register.

CHAPTER 5

Conclusion

The informal and HTT sectors remain tantalizing prospects for revenue authorities seeking to expand the tax base and raise their revenue-to-GDP ratio. This publication draws on lessons from international data and experiences to provide the following key recommendations.

- **Harness data and technology effectively to improve enforcement.** Successfully taxing the informal and HTT sectors begins with measurement. Policymakers need to produce periodic, reliable estimates of underreported liabilities, exempt activities, and unregistered entities that are aligned with revenue potential. Generic estimates of informal activity are not indicative of the sector's revenue potential or of its current contributions to tax revenue. This publication proposes a system of smart enforcement, which can regularly produce tax gap estimates, identify informal firms, and help governments maximize the efficiency of risk-based audits.

- **Taxpayer registration drives do not provide value for money.** Drives to increase tax registration are highly cost-ineffective and may in fact counter efforts to reduce evasion and avoidance among registered entities. There is little evidence that expanding tax registration, particularly to smaller taxpayers, raises revenue or brings nontax benefits to the newly registered.

- **Presumptive tax regimes can increase revenue, but the threshold must be set carefully.** Presumptive tax regimes perform better both in terms of raising revenue and doing so at a reasonable level of administrative and compliance costs. By simplifying tax calculations and using proxies such as turnover, land size, or number of employees, these regimes make it easier for small businesses and HTT sectors to comply with tax obligations. They reduce the burden on tax authorities by minimizing the need for detailed audits and complex recordkeeping while ensuring a steady stream of revenue. Additionally, presumptive taxes help bring informal firms into the tax net without imposing excessive costs, creating a pathway toward full formalization. However, to maximize their effectiveness, such regimes must be carefully designed to avoid overburdening smaller firms and must be paired with robust enforcement and regular evaluation to ensure fairness and efficiency in implementation.

- **Targeted outreach and education programs can help reach the hard-to-tax sectors.** HTT sectors like agriculture and small business professionals require a tailored approach to address their unique challenges effectively. These sectors often operate with irregular income patterns, rely heavily on cash transactions, and lack robust bookkeeping practices, making traditional tax enforcement mechanisms less effective. For agriculture, land-based taxes or output-based presumptive taxes can simplify compliance and capture income indirectly. For professionals, linking tax compliance to licensing requirements, promoting digital payment systems, and implementing withholding taxes on payments can help ensure better coverage. Additionally, targeted education and outreach programs can build trust and improve voluntary compliance within these sectors. Tailored strategies that account for the specific characteristics of each HTT group are essential to expanding the tax base sustainably and equitably.

- **Devote resources to removing inactive and possibly fraudulent taxpayers from tax registers.** The rise of VATs around the world, particularly in low- and middle-income countries, has fundamentally reshaped our understanding of taxable activities and underscored the importance of maintaining a clean tax register. The VAT's unique design ensures that a significant portion of economic activity is taxed indirectly through its withholding mechanism, even in the informal sector that traditionally escapes direct taxation. The shift toward VAT, however, also heightens the need to maintain an accurate and up-to-date tax register as fraudulent, ghost firms break into the system to facilitate fraudulent claims of input tax credits and refunds.

APPENDIX

Data Sources

Data in this publication come from the following sources:

- **International Labour Organization:** Data on informal employment for 2000–2023 are sourced from the International Labour Organization (ILO). The dataset includes detailed statistics on informal employment disaggregated by gender and across various economies. The data are publicly accessible through the organization's website and database platforms. With its longitudinal coverage and granularity, this dataset is an invaluable resource for understanding the evolution of informal employment globally.[1]
- **World Development Indicators:** Data on gross domestic product, population, and other economic and developmental indicators is sourced from the World Bank's World Development Indicators, 1960–present. The indicators provide country-level data on topics such as gross domestic product, tax revenue, employment, business environment, and poverty, making it a critical resource for analyzing economic trends and policy impacts. The dataset is updated annually and can be accessed through the World Bank's online data portal.[2]
- **World Governance Indicators:** Data on governance-related metrics is drawn from the World Governance Indicators, an authoritative dataset compiled by the World Bank for over 200 economies from 1996 onward, covering six key dimensions of governance: (i) voice and accountability, (ii) political stability and absence of violence, (iii) government effectiveness, (iv) regulatory quality, (v) rule of law, and (vi) control of corruption. The indicators are derived from diverse sources, including surveys, expert assessments, and administrative data, ensuring a comprehensive and nuanced view of governance quality. The data are publicly available through the World Bank's data portal.[3]

---

1 These data were downloaded from ILO. Informal Economy. in November 2024.

2 These data were downloaded from World Bank. World Development Indicators. in November 2024.

3 These data were downloaded from World Bank. Worldwide Governance Indicators. in November 2024.

- **Global Findex Database:** Data on financial inclusion is sourced from the Global Findex Database, a comprehensive dataset developed by the World Bank. The database provides detailed insights into how individuals in more than 140 economies access and use financial services, including accounts, savings, credit, payments, and financial technology. Covering data from 2011, 2014, 2017, and 2021, the database allows for trend analysis and international comparisons. The data are collected through nationally representative surveys of adults and are freely accessible via the World Bank's data portal.[4]

[4] These data were downloaded from World Bank. The Global Findex Database 2021. in November 2024.

BIBLIOGRAPHY

Alm, J. R., J. Martinez-Vazquez, and S. Wallace. 2005. *Taxing the Hard-to-Tax: Lessons from Theory and Practice.* Emerald Group Publishing Limited.

Almunia, M., J. Hjort, J. Knebelmann, and L. Tian. 2024. Strategic or Confused Firms? Evidence from "Missing" Transactions in Uganda. The *Review of Economics and Statistics*. 106 (1). pp. 256–265.

Anyidoho, N. A., M. Gallien, M. Rogan, and V. Van Den Boogaard. 2025. The Taxed Informal Economy: Fiscal Burdens and Inequality in Accra. *World Development*. 187. 106879.

Barnwal, P., J. I. Dingel, D. Iurchenko, P. Krishna, and E. Van Leemput. 2024. Internal Trade Barriers in India. *Working Paper*. Unpublished.

Barwahwala, T., A. Mahajan, S. Mittal, and O. Reich. 2024. Is Model Accuracy Enough? A Field Evaluation of a Machine Learning Model to Catch Bogus Firms. *ACM Journal on Computing and Sustainable Societies*. 2 (3). pp. 1–43.

Bashir, M., U. Jamal, K. Mcnabb, and M. Waseem. 2024a. Intended and Unintended Consequences of Anti-Avoidance Rules: Evidence from Uganda. *University of Manchester Working Paper*.

Bashir, M., Z. Farooq, U. Jamal, and M. Waseem. 2024b. Size-Based Policies and Firm Growth: Evidence from Pakistan. *University of Manchester Working Paper*.

Benhassine, N., D. Mckenzie, V. Pouliquen, and M. Santini. 2018. Does Inducing Informal Firms to Formalize Make Sense? Experimental Evidence from Benin. *Journal of Public Economics*. 157. pp. 1–14.

Bergolo, M. and G. Cruces. 2021. The Anatomy of Behavioral Responses to Social Assistance When Informal Employment Is High. *Journal of Public Economics*. 193. 104313.

Besley, T. and T. Persson. 2014. Why Do Developing Countries Tax So Little? *Journal of Economic* Perspectives. 28 (4). pp. 99–120.

Best, M., J. Shah, and M. Waseem. 2021. Detection Without Deterrence: Tax Audits with Limited Fiscal Capacity. *University of Manchester Working Paper.*

Best, M. C., A. Brockmeyer, H. J. Kleven, J. Spinnewijn, and M. Waseem. 2015. Production Versus Revenue Efficiency with Limited Tax Capacity: Theory and Evidence from Pakistan. *Journal of Political Economy*. 123 (6). pp. 1311–1355.

Boning, W. C., N. Hendren, B. Sprung-Keyser, and E. Stuart. 2025. A Welfare Analysis of Tax Audits Across the Income Distribution. *The Quarterly Journal of Economics*. 140 (1). pp. 63–112.

Brockmeyer, A. and M. Hernandez. 2021. Taxation, Information and Withholding: Evidence from Costa Rica. *Policy Research Working Paper*. No. 7600. World Bank.

Brockmeyer, A., G. Mascagni, V. Nair, M. Waseem, and M. Almunia. 2024. Does the Value-Added Tax Add Value? Lessons Using Administrative Data from a Diverse Set of Countries. *Journal of Economic Perspectives*. 38 (1). pp. 107–132.

Bruhn, M. and J. Loeprick. 2016. Small Business Tax Policy and Informality: Evidence from Georgia. *International Tax and Public Finance*. 23. pp. 834–853.

Buettner, T. and A. Tassi. 2023. VAT Fraud and Reverse Charge: Empirical Evidence from VAT Return Data. *International Tax and Public Finance*. 30 (3). pp. 849–878.

Campos, F., M. P. Goldstein, and D. J. Mckenzie. 2015. Short-Term Impacts of Formalization Assistance and a Bank Information Session on Business Registration and Access to Finance in Malawi. *Policy Research Working Paper*. No. 7183. World Bank Group.

Carrillo, P., D. Pomeranz, and M. Singhal. 2017. Dodging the Taxman: Firm Misreporting and Limits to Tax Enforcement. *American Economic Journal: Applied Economics*. 9 (2). pp. 144–164.

Carrillo, P., D. Donaldson, D. Pomeranz, and M. Singhal. 2023. Ghosting the Tax Authority: Fake Firms and Tax Fraud in Ecuador. *American Economic Review: Insights*. 5 (4). pp. 427–444.

Choudhary, K. and B. Gupta. 2024. Dynamics of Firm Growth Around Tax Thresholds: Evidence from India. *Working Paper of the Max Planck Institute for Tax Law and Public Finance*. No. 2024-05.

De Andrade, G. H., M. Bruhn, and D. Mckenzie. 2014. A Helping Hand or the Long Arm of the Law? Experimental Evidence on What Governments Can Do to Formalize Firms. *The World Bank Economic Review*. 30 (1). pp. 24–54.

De Giorgi, G. and A. Rahman. 2013. SMEs Registration: Evidence from an RCT in Bangladesh. *Economics Letters*. 120 (3). pp. 573–578.

De Mel, S., D. Mckenzie, and C. Woodruff. 2013. The Demand for, and Consequences of, Formalization Among Informal Firms in Sri Lanka. *American Economic Journal: Applied Economics*. 5 (2). pp. 122–50.

De Paula, A. and J. A. Scheinkman. 2010. Value-Added Taxes, Chain Effects, and Informality. *American Economic Journal: Macroeconomics*. 2 (4). pp. 195–221.

Dwenger, N. and L. Treber. 2022. Shaming for Tax Enforcement. *Management Science*. 68 (11). pp. 8202–8233.

Dzansi, J., A. Jensen, D. Lagakos, and H. Telli. 2022. Technology and Tax Capacity: Evidence from Local Governments in Ghana. National *Bureau of Economic Research Working Paper Series*. No. 29923. National Bureau of Economic Research.

Elgin, C., M. A. Kose, F. Ohnsorge, and S. Yu. 2021. Understanding Informality. CEPR Discussion Paper. No. 16497. CEPR Press.

Fajnzylber, P., W. F. Maloney, and G. V. Montes-Rojas. 2011. Does Formality Improve Micro-Firm Performance? Evidence From the Brazilian SIMPLES Program. *Journal of Development Economics*. 94 (2). pp. 262–276.

Farooq, Z., O. Ur Rehman, and M. Waseem. 2024. Predistribution Vs. Redistribution: The Role of Taxes, Transfers, and Public Spending in Reducing Inequality. Unpublished.

Gadenne, L., T. K. Nandi, and R. Rathelot. 2024. Taxation and Supplier Networks: Evidence from India. *Institute for Fiscal Studies Working Papers*. No. W19/21. Institute for Fiscal Studies.

Gallien, M., G. Occhiali, and V. Van Den Boogaard. 2023. Catch Them If You Can: The Politics and Practice of a Taxpayer Registration Exercise. *ICTD Working Paper*. No. 160.

Gallien, M., G. Mascagni, M. Moore, et al. 2023. Why Mass Tax Registration Campaigns Do Not Work. International Center for Tax and Development Policy Brief 2. Institute of Development Studies.

Garriga, P. and D. Tortarolo. 2024. Firms as Tax Collectors. *Journal of Public Economics*. 233. 105092.

Gebresilasse, M. M. and S. Sow. 2020. Effect of VAT Adoption on Manufacturing Firms in Ethiopia. *International Journal of Economics and Finance*. 12 (10).

Government of India, Ministry of Finance. 2018. Economic Survey 2017–18. Volume I.

Government of India, Ministry of Finance, Press Information Bureau. 2024. 29,273 Bogus Firms Involved in Suspected Input Tax Credit (ITC) Evasion of Rs. 44,015 Crore Detected in a Sustained Drive Against Non-Existent Taxpayers by GST Formations Across the Country Since May 2023; 121 Arrested. News release. 7 January.

Government of Pakistan, Federal Board of Revenue. 2022. *Tax Gap Report 2022*.

Harju, J., T. Matikka, and T. Rauhanen. 2019. Compliance Costs vs. Tax Incentives: Why Do Entrepreneurs Respond to Size-Based Regulations? *Journal of Public Economics*. 173. pp. 139–164.

Hoy, C., T. Scot, A. Oguso, et al. 2024. Trade-Offs in the Design of Simplified Tax Regimes: Evidence from Sub-Saharan Africa. *Policy Research Working Paper*. 10909. World Bank.

Joshi, A., W. Prichard, and C. Heady. 2014. Taxing the Informal Economy: The Current State of Knowledge and Agendas for Future Research. *The Journal of Development Studies*. 50 (10). pp. 1325–1347.

Jouste, M., M. I. Nalukwago, and R. Waiswa. 2021. Do Tax Administrative Interventions Targeted at Small Businesses Improve Tax Compliance and Revenue Collection? Evidence from Ugandan Administrative Tax Data. *WIDER Working Paper*. No. 17/2021. UNU-WIDER.

Keen, M. 2008. VAT, Tariffs, and Withholding: Border Taxes and Informality in Developing Countries. *Journal of Public Economics*. 92. pp. 1892–1906.

Keen, M. and J. Mintz. 2004. The Optimal Threshold for a Value-Added Tax. *Journal of Public Economics*. 88 (3-4). pp. 559–576.

Keen, M. and J. Slemrod. 2017. Optimal Tax Administration. *Journal of Public Economics*. 152. pp. 133–142.

Keen, M. and S. Smith. 2006. VAT Fraud and Evasion: What Do We Know and What Can Be Done? *National Tax Journal*. pp. 861–887.

Kleven, H. J. and M. Waseem. 2013. Using Notches to Uncover Optimization Frictions and Structural Elasticities: Theory and Evidence from Pakistan. *Quarterly Journal of Economics*. 128 (2). pp. 669–723.

Kleven, H. J., M. B. Knudsen, C. T. Kreiner, et al. 2011. Unwilling or Unable to Cheat? Evidence From a Tax Audit Experiment in Denmark. *Econometrica*. 79 (3). pp. 651–692.

Kleven, H. J., C. T. Kreiner, and E. Saez. 2016. Why Can Modern Governments Tax So Much? An Agency Model of Firms as Fiscal Intermediaries. *Economica*. 83 (330). pp. 219–246.

Lediga, C., N. Riedel, and K. Strohmaier. 2025. What You Do (Not) Get When Expanding the Net—Evidence from Forced Taxpayer Registrations in South Africa. *Journal of Development Economics*. 172. p. 103388.

Liu, L., B. Lockwood, and E. Tam. 2022. Small Firm Growth and the VAT Threshold: Evidence for the UK. *IMF Working Paper*. No. 2024/033.

Luttmer, E. F. P. and M. Singhal. 2014. Tax Morale. *Journal of Economic Perspectives*. 28 (4). pp. 149–168.

Mahajan, A., S. Mittal, O. Reich, and T. Barwahwala. 2024. Using Machine Learning to Catch Bogus Firms.

Mascagni, G., F. Santoro, D. Mukama, J. Karangwa, and N. Hakizimana. 2022. Active Ghosts: Nil-filing in Rwanda. *World Development*. 152. p. 105806.

Mckenzie, D. and Y. S. Sakho. 2010. Does It Pay Firms to Register for Taxes? The Impact of Formality on Firm Profitability. *Journal of Development Economics.* 91 (1). pp. 15–24.

Milanez, A. 2017. Legal Tax Liability, Legal Remittance Responsibility and Tax Incidence: Three Dimensions of Business Taxation. *OECD Taxation Working Papers.* No. 32. OECD Publishing.

Mittal, S., O. Reich, and A. Mahajan. 2018. Who Is Bogus? Using One-Sided Labels to Identify Fraudulent Firms from Tax Returns. *Proceedings of the 1st ACM SIGCAS Conference on Computing and Sustainable Societies.* pp. 1–11.

Monteiro, J. C. M. and J. J. Assuncao. 2012. Coming Out of the Shadows? Estimating the Impact of Bureaucracy Simplification and Tax Cut on Formality in Brazilian Microenterprises. *Journal of Development Economics.* 99 (1). pp 105–115.

Naritomi, J. 2019. Consumers as Tax Auditors. *American Economic Review.* 109 (9). pp. 3031–72.

Ogembo, D. 2019. Are Presumptive Taxes a Good Option for Taxing Self-Employed Professionals in Low & Middle-Income Countries? *Journal of Tax Administration.* 5 (2).

———. 2022. Trust or Power: Improving Tax Compliance by Self-Employed Professionals. *Intertax.* 50 (2).

Okunogbe, O. 2021. Becoming Legible to the State. *World Bank Policy Research Working Paper.* No. 9852.

Okunogbe, O. and V. Pouliquen. 2022. Technology, Taxation, and Corruption: Evidence from the Introduction of Electronic *Tax Filing. American Economic Journal: Economic Policy*. 14 (1). p. 341–72.

Okunogbe, O. and G. Tourek. 2024. How Can Lower-Income Countries Collect More Taxes? The Role of Technology, Tax Agents, and Politics. *Journal of Economic Perspectives.* 38 (1). pp. 81–106.

Pomeranz, D. 2015. No Taxation Without Information: Deterrence and Self-Enforcement in the Value Added Tax. *American Economic Review.* 105 (8). pp. 2539–2569.

Rinaudo, M. 2015. *Bangladesh Technical Assistance Report: Methodology to Measure the Value Added Tax Gap in Bangladesh.* World Bank.

Rocha, R., G. Ulyssea, and L. Rachter. 2018. Do Lower Taxes Reduce Informality? Evidence from Brazil. *Journal of Development Economics.* 134. pp. 28–49.

Rothenberg, A. D., A. Gaduh, N. E. Burger, et al. 2016. Rethinking Indonesia's Informal Sector. *World Development.* 80. pp. 96–113.

Shukla, G. P., D. M. Pham, M. Engelschalk, and T. M. Le. 2011. *Tax Reform in Vietnam: Toward a More Efficient and Equitable System*. World Bank.

Slemrod, J. and T. Velayudhan. 2018. Do Firms Remit at Least 85% of Tax Everywhere? New Evidence from India. Journal of *Tax Administration*. 4 (1). pp. 24–37.

———. 2022. The VAT at 100: A Retrospective Survey and Agenda for Future Research. *Public Finance Review*. 50 (1). pp. 4–32.

Slemrod, J., O. Ur Rehman, and M. Waseem. 2022. How Do Taxpayers Respond to Public Disclosure and Social Recognition Programs? Evidence from Pakistan. *The Review of Economics and Statistics*. 104 (1). pp. 116–132.

Thanh, S. D., T. T. Bui, and T. T. Kien. 2014. Reforms of Tax System in Vietnam: Toward International Integration Commitments Until 2020.

Tourek, G. 2022. Targeting in Tax Behavior: Evidence from Rwandan. *Journal of Development Economics*. 158. p. 102911.

Ulyssea, G. 2010. Regulation of Entry, Labor Market Institutions and the Informal Sector. *Journal of Development Economics*. 91 (1). pp. 87–99.

———. 2021. Informality and Taxation in Developing Asia. ADB Background Paper.

Waseem, M. 2018. Taxes, Informality and Income Shifting: Evidence from a Recent Pakistani Tax Reform. *Journal of Public Economics*. 157. pp. 41–77.

———. 2020a. Does Cutting the Tax Rate to Zero Induce Behavior Different from Other Tax Cuts? Evidence from Pakistan. *The Review of Economics and Statistics*. 102 (3). pp. 426–441.

———. 2020b. The Role of Withholding in the Self-Enforcement of a Value-Added Tax: Evidence from Pakistan. *The Review of Economics and Statistics*. pp. 1–44.

———. 2023. Overclaimed Refunds, Undeclared Sales, and Invoice Mills: Nature and Extent of Noncompliance in a Value-Added Tax. *Journal of Public Economics*. 218. p. 104783.

Zolt, E. M. and R. M. Bird. 2005. Redistribution via Taxation: The Limited Role of the Personal Income Tax in Developing Countries. *UCLA Law Review*. 52. pp. 5–22.

www.ingramcontent.com/pod-product-compliance
Lightning Source LLC
Chambersburg PA
CBHW041757220926
51847CB00014B/239